Aftershock

All things fall and are built again,
And those that build them again are gay.
W. B. Yeats

Ellen Wolfe

AFTERSHOCK

THE STORY OF A PSYCHOTIC EPISODE

G. P. Putnam's Sons, New York

The events in this book are true; all names and identification have been changed throughout.

For
D. L.
B. B. S.

FIVE YEARS ago I spent a month in a psychiatric hospital being treated for a psychotic episode. I was thirty-five years old at the time, the wife of a photographer, the mother of two small children.

The episode was a tremendous shock to me. I had been seeing a psychiatrist off and on for a number of years. But my neuroses had not been crippling ones. I had no obvious symptoms: no tics, no phobias, no compulsions, no irrational fears. I did not have anxiety attacks. I was not frigid. I was not given to hysterics. I did have frequent depressions and feelings of inadequacy. Like almost all neurotic people, I had too an abnormal hunger for affection and an abnormal sensitivity to rejection, hostility, or even a mild rebuke.

But I had always managed to wear a façade of normality. I had done well in school and received raises and promotions regularly when I worked. I had married a handsome and talented man. I had numerous friends; and had, through treatment, become more self-assured, less de-

pendent on others for approval. I had learned how to express anger and how to evaluate myself more realistically.

I had stopped seeing my psychiatrist because I thought that I had made considerable progress and no longer needed him. I knew that I loved my husband and my children and felt that I was a fairly good wife and mother. I knew also that I was tense with the children and overly fatigued by caring for them, but this I considered a temporary problem. There were, I told myself, a few difficult years to be got through until the children were in school. Life would be better when they were older.

And then one day in June I woke up in a hospital . . .

WHERE AM I?" I heard my voice ask, and as I asked it, I thought: What a strange thing to have to ask. Why don't I *know* where I am?

A nurse was standing beside me. I was lying on a bed or a stretcher. (Even now I don't know where I was then. The treatment room? The recovery room? My own room in the hospital?) She told me the name of the hospital. I heard her but did not look at her. I looked at the ceiling of the room. It was low, white, smoothly plastered, as blank as my mind. The name meant nothing: I had never heard of the hospital.

"Why?" I asked. "Why am I here?"

"You had a nervous breakdown." Her voice had a familiar tone. Had I had any memory then, I might have thought: That's exactly the tone of voice I use to answer my son's questions. But he is only two years old and I am thirty-five. I did not think this, however. My thoughts were simple. They crossed my mind in single file.

"Nervous breakdown?"

"Yes."

Silence. I continued to look at the ceiling and tried
to think. Nervous breakdown. I more or less knew what
the term meant. When I was little, nervous ladies had
nervous breakdowns and disappeared from the neighborhood for a few months and the ladies who remained on their front galleries and in their gardens
discussed the missing ladies in low voices whenever they
thought there were no children around or listening.
Ambitious, overworked men sometimes have breakdowns. But I could not connect myself with the term.
Something must *happen* when you have a breakdown.
I could not remember anything unusual having happened to me. I had merely awakened, as though from
a dream, to find myself lying on a hospital bed, with a
nurse beside me.

I was seated on my bed in my hospital room. There
were two beds in the room. One was mine; the other was
unoccupied. The walls of the room were a pale green
that was someone's idea of a noninstitutional shade. The
door of the room had a small pane of glass set into it at
eye level. On the table beside my bed was a vase of zinnias: bright yellow, orange, and red; robust colors that
seemed out of place in a hospital where people were
sick, perhaps even dying. I looked down at my feet and
studied my slippers: pale-blue terrycloth scuffs, badly in
need of a washing. I did not recognize them. I had never
seen them before—although as I thought this, I realized

that it was unlikely that the hospital had provided them. They must belong to me, I decided.

The door of the room swung open and a man entered: my husband, David. I knew him at once, although I had not thought of him at all since awakening some time before (how long before I do not know) to ask, "Where am I?"

"Darling!" I jumped up from my bed and hurried across the room. I rested my head on his left shoulder and encircled his waist with my arms.

"Careful! You'll crush the flowers," he said, but he smiled as he said it.

I backed away and looked into his eyes, not at the roses he was carrying. I had already glanced at them. They were tiny pink buds, the kind of roses a bashful young man might give his sweetheart. They did not seem appropriate for a woman who had "broken down." They did not interest me except for their symbolic value. *I still love you,* the gift implied, but I looked for the truth in his eyes. They smiled at me. I liked the laugh lines that fanned out from their corners.

"Darling! Darling!" Clinging to him again, I closed my eyes, and together we swayed for a moment until he released me.

"I'll ask the nurse for a vase . . . how are you? You seem much better."

"Better than what? I feel as though I just woke up. What happened? I don't understand . . ."

"You will—wait—I'll be right back."

He left the room, carrying the roses. I sat down on my bed. My left hand reached for a package of Kool cigarettes that was lying on the bedside table, next to the zinnias. I shook out a cigarette, placed it between my lips, picked up a folder of matches, and lit the cigarette. The matchbook was brown with white lettering: THE ALGONQUIN HOTEL. Where did the matchbook come from? I had not been there for years. David doesn't go there. I drew deeply on my cigarette, then blew the smoke out. I looked at the cigarette between my fingers. My actions of lighting it and smoking it seemed entirely independent of my own volition. Then it occurred to me: I do not smoke. I quit when I was twenty-one. I never smoke—not even at cocktail parties. Why am I smoking a cigarette now? My hand moved the cigarette to my mouth; again I inhaled, then exhaled the smoke in a small, steady stream.

The door opened and David came in again. He placed the vase of roses beside the zinnias. There was scarcely room for both vases. The zinnias seemed to overpower the rosebuds. He had brought the rosebuds, but where had the zinnias come from?

David sat down on the bed, near me. I inhaled again. I felt a little dizzy, just nicely light-headed. "Do I smoke, Dave? Why am I smoking now?"

"Well, you never used to . . . you started the day you came here . . . you said there was nothing else to do . . ."

"How long have I been here?"

"Three weeks today."

"Three weeks! But why haven't you been to see me?"

A look of pain replaced the half-smile that he had been wearing. He reached for my hand, cleared his throat, then hesitated, as though unsure of what to say. "I—I've come every day—every single, solitary day. I've brought you flowers—every day."

I stubbed out the cigarette in a small green metal ashtray. What he had said did not make any sense. Was it possible that I was dreaming, that I would wake up to find that I was not in the hospital after all? But the ashtray felt solid and real and cool to my touch; the smoke from my cigarette hung in the air; there was a trace of whiskey on my husband's breath, and the skin on his cheeks and jaws was pinpricked by his beard. I knew that it was not a dream.

"I can't remember. How did I get here? What happened?"

"But you know who I am?"

I laughed at him. "Of course! You're my husband. Why do you ask such a silly question?"

"Do you remember the children?"

I had to think. It was as though someone had asked me a casual question, say, about a book I had read some years before: "Have you ever read *Ethan Frome?*" "*Ethan Frome?*" I might reply. "Let's see, that's Edith Wharton, isn't it—he was crippled—he drove a sled into a tree—"

In the same way, I had to search my memory for my children. After a moment, an image came to mind. "Of course, Larry—"

"And Beth?"

"Beth? I don't have a daughter." It seemed to me a foolish conversation. I certainly ought to know whether I had a daughter or not.

"Elizabeth. You call her Beth—and sometimes Betsy."

Suddenly I realized he was right. I did have a daughter. Yet I could not picture her face.

Silence. He looked at me and his expression was a mixture of worry, tenderness, caution. I released my hand from his hold and crossed the room to stand beside the window. There was no view: the blinds were closed.

His voice followed me: "You have pictures of them both. At first you looked at them all the time."

I turned around. "Why don't I remember anything!" I was surprised at the shrillness of my voice.

"You're having shock treatment. It makes you forget. Don't worry. It will all come back. You'll remember everything."

"How do you know?"

"The doctors told me. And, darling, you're so much better already."

"Where are the pictures? I want to see them."

"In your wallet, I guess. Where is your bag?"

"I don't know."

"It's probably in the closet." He got up and started toward a long narrow metal cabinet on the wall opposite my bed. I reached the cabinet before he did and opened the door. Two of my dresses were hanging there: one was green linen; the other was orange seersucker. I recognized that they belonged to me. My black patent leather hatbox was on the floor of the cabinet. A black straw clutch bag leaned against the hatbox. I stood before the open door and stared down at the bag.

"There it is—on the floor."

"That's not my bag."

"Yes, it is. You bought it just before you came here."

He must be right, I thought. If he says it is mine, I suppose it is. I stooped down and picked it up, opened it, and found proof of the truth of his words: *my* green leather wallet, *my* Swiss comb, *my* Hazel Bishop lipsticks: Real, Real Pink and Real, Real Orange. But it was odd to find all these things in a bag I had never seen before.

Together we sat on the bed and looked at the pictures. There were two of them, both creased and dog-eared from being carried about in my wallet. In one, my small son was crawling on a bed. (So that is what my bed looks like. It was a sensory impression, rather than a thought. My eyes *knew* when they saw that rumpled Madras bedspread that it was the one I nightly removed from the bed, folded, and hung over the chair at the desk.) A hair roller poked idiotically from my son's mouth. His eyes were smiling.

"He's beautiful!"

"That's what you always say."

"Well, isn't he?"

"Yes, of course."

The second picture—but how could I have forgotten that plump baby body, that curly brown hair that hung down into her eyes because she would not sit still for us to cut it, that chubby hand, here reaching toward the camera, other times, all times, reaching for whatever she had not already held in her inquisitive grasp?

"Oh, she's beautiful, too. Oh, darling, let's have another baby!"

"We'll see. When you're all well, we'll talk about it."

I had looked at the pictures and found my children—but I was with them only in a moment suspended in time. I had no past; I had no future; I had no thoughts of home, no normal maternal worries. It did not occur to me to ask who was taking care of my children while I was in the hospital. I existed only in that room, sitting on that bed. My husband sitting beside me and my children somewhere were the only other people in the world, as I then knew it. I was neither happy nor sad. I merely *was*—or at least that is the way I remember that moment.

Awakened from sleep by the chirping of a nurse, I turned over to see what she wanted of me. She was young and pretty; her uniform fit snugly around her narrow waist. She held the thermometer toward me, and as I reached for it, I was conscious of my hair: it frowzed about my face. Her dark brown hair was neatly caught back by her starched cap.

I put the tip of the thermometer in my mouth.

"No! No! Not there!"

Embarrassed—because I never liked to be corrected—I removed it from my mouth and slid it into my rectum. She waited. I dozed.

"All right. Take it out."

I did so.

"No breakfast for you this morning," her voice announced. I was drifting off to sleep, unmoved by her words. "You're having a treatment."

When later, much later, I woke up again, my stomach demanded its food: it grumbled as I combed my hair and smeared makeup over my face and painted my lips with Real, Real Pink. I wandered out to the dining room and sat down with the other patients, envying them their toast and cereal and eggs. I smoked a cigarette and listened to the conversation, mostly about nothing.

"My coffee is cold already. Why do they bring it with your eggs? I like it after," someone complained.

The fat girl was still hungry after she had finished her breakfast. "May I have some more toast and jelly?" It was brought to her, but still she was not satisfied. She eyed the small square container of grape jelly that lay unopened on the plate of the nun, who was the fat girl's special friend. (Why did I know that the nun and the fat girl were friends, but not know why I was in the hospital or how long I had been there?)

"Aren't you going to eat your jelly?" the girl asked.

"You may have it," the nun said, handing it to her.

The nun's face too was plump, but not unpleasantly so. It was plump and placid. Her skin was smooth and almost without wrinkles, although she appeared to be in her forties. I wondered why she was in the hospital. If she could not find peace of mind in the orderly existence of the convent, how were the rest of us supposed to manage in the chaos we call civilization? The fat girl hung around her all the time. The nun was kind to her. It was impossible to tell from her waxen face whether she liked the fat girl or merely tolerated her.

I was hungry, and irritable because I was hungry. I disliked the fat girl because she was loud and greedy. I disliked the old woman down the hall who moaned throughout the day and most of the night. I was indifferent to her suffering and only wished she would stop making all that noise, which became more and more intrusive as I sat and waited for someone to take me off for my treatment.

My treatment. The words had no connotations for me. Even the more explicit term "shock treatment" failed to shock me. We patients discussed it casually: "Are you having shock treatments?" "Yes, I'm having one today." I didn't wonder at all about what would happen to me during the treatment or why I needed it. It was merely something that occurred at regular intervals: a part of the hospital routine.

When the others had finished breakfast, I went with them to the dayroom. I can remember nothing about that room except that I spent a lot of time there. It must have been a large room with many sofas and chairs and tables. Probably some magazines were laid out on the tables. Perhaps there was a television set. One thing I do remember is sitting in a chair and leafing through a *New Yorker* until my name was called out by a nurse. When I looked up I recognized the aide who had just entered the room. He was the one who always took me to my treatments. I was quite willing to go with him. I was willing to go anywhere to escape from that room, where there was nothing to do but idle through magazines.

The aide was a tall young Negro man, so tall that his body was shaped into a stoop from years of hunching down to hear what others had to say. His skin was light and his voice was gentle.

"Come on, Miz Wolfe, it's time to go." He held my arm lightly as we walked down the hallway, and I did not mind, even though I was aware of the implication that I might suddenly turn unruly. His hold continued gentle all the way down the corridor to the locked door that separated the patients' rooms from the small corridor containing the elevator. He released my arm, unlocked the door, then locked it behind us after I had docilely preceded him through the doorway.

I liked him. He looked strong, yet kind. I smiled at him as he took my arm again and led me to the elevator.

"You feeling good today," he said, returning my smile.

"Sure," I answered. "Why not?"

"That's the spirit. They ain't nothing in the world worth worrying about."

I agreed. I was totally at peace with myself and as much of the world as I then knew.

We left the elevator, and he ushered me into a small waiting room adjacent to the treatment room. Why do I remember the bright blue spreads on the two couches in that room but nothing at all of the dayroom? Perhaps because I was aware as I sat down on one of the couches that those very spreads were often advertised in magazines like *Mademoiselle* for use in college rooms. I even remembered the name of the pattern: Piping Rock. It seemed to me amusing that spreads usually shown in rooms hung with college pennants and occupied by models posing as All-American college girls should be here where a group of psychiatric patients sat and conversed in splinters. In my mind I tried writing another kind of headline for the spreads: BATES: BEST OF ALL SPREADS FOR THE BATTY. But I was diverted from this game by the young man who sat on the opposite couch.

He was a handsome man with thick, black wavy hair, but his eyes were fierce as he demanded to know my name.

"Why do you want to know my name?" I asked.

"Why don't you want to tell me your name?"

"I didn't say I didn't want to tell you. I merely asked why you wanted to know."

"That's the same thing, isn't it?"

"No, not at all."

"Well, listen, *honey*"—his tone was heavily sarcastic; clearly, I was not his idea of honey, not his cup of tea at all—"if you think I give one damn what your name is, you're *crazy!*"

I stared at him. He slumped so badly that I couldn't tell whether he was tall or short. I wondered why he was so angry. The young man and I remained silent. He didn't look at me. The other waiting patient, a middle-aged man with a bald head and large, sad brown eyes, sat with his legs widespread, shoulders hunched forward, hands dangling between his legs. He too was silent.

A nurse entered and beckoned to me. "The doctor is here."

I got up and followed her out to the hall. I lay down on a stretcher and was wheeled into the treatment room. I had no curiosity about the apparatus in the room. There were perhaps three or four people in the room: nurses, doctors, interns—I didn't attempt to sort them out. The only one who interested me was *my* doctor. I didn't know his name, but I knew that I had seen him before.

He grinned as he bent over me. Brown eyes coming closer, closer. His grin splitting his face wide open. His boyish head bobbing before me.

"Hi!"

"Hi!"

We sounded like people meeting at a party.

On my right, someone was preparing an injection. I continued to smile, but my body tensed at the approach of the needle.

"Ouch!"

Then the delicious voluptuousness of falling from consciousness. My field of vision narrowed rapidly. What remained blurred, then faded away. When I woke up in the recovery room, again I had to ask, "Where am I?"

Another visit from David. More flowers. This time they were gladiolas. Yellow. He must have been in such a rush to get there that he grabbed the first thing the florist suggested. He hates gladiolas, and I am not especially fond of them. I was getting bored with the ritual of looking pleased with his flowers. I was so bored. Why didn't they let me go home? I asked David if he please wouldn't do something about shortening my stay. "Tell them you think I should go home."

"I'm not a doctor, dear. I have to listen to them, do what they think is right."

"Well, you could try. You're not even willing to try. Tell them the children need me."

"Ah, so you remember that you have *two* children today."

I didn't understand his remark, not remembering then that once I had forgotten my daughter. "Of course I remember the children, and I'm sure they need me."

"They *do* need you—we all miss you."

"Then let me go home." It was all so simple and logical. I wanted to go home. I was wanted and needed at home. I should therefore be allowed to go home. One and one equals two. What was the matter with those people that they couldn't see that?

David tried to change the subject: "Look. I brought a job I just did to show you." He opened an envelope and slid out a photograph. I glanced at it: a close-up of a woman's hand—long, perfectly shaped rosy nails, a wide gold wedding band. For a hand lotion account, no doubt.

"Mmmmm. Very nice. Well, when *can* I go home?"

"In a few days. Don't you like the photograph?"

"Yes, sure I like it. Why not now?"

David sighed but kept his expression steady as a beacon. "I just told you: it's not up to me to decide." The beacon swept across the room, then back again. (Look at *me*, Dave, look at *me*. Don't look at the room, look at me. *I want to go home!*)

He walked over and picked up a potted plant. Philodendron, dying. "I can't wait to get to the country and start growing things. Pots! Plants can't grow in pots. The first thing I'm going to do is get some good tools and get to work on the garden—they've got nothing but junk in there now."

"I wish I had the slightest idea what you were talking about."

He wheeled around to face me. I was sitting on the side of the bed, swinging my legs back and forth. "You don't remember the house?"

"What house?"

"We're buying a house in the country. Near Jane. An old farmhouse."

I wanted to please him. He has such a nice steady smile. Even when he is not really smiling, it seems to hover on his face, like an afterglow. If I tell him I still don't remember, will it fade away? Abruptly, I jumped down from the bed. "I found a picture in my wallet. Of a house I've never seen. Is it ours?" I had reached my bag and was rummaging through the wallet, looking for the picture.

"You have a picture of the house, yes."

"Here it is. How odd. I looked at this picture yesterday and couldn't think why I had it." I looked at the picture again, more carefully. A farmhouse, with two lines of shuttered windows, set regular as bean rows, across the front of the house. Thick old shade trees. A picket fence. A rope hammock hung between two trees. A nice, old-fashioned place that made you think of lemonade and collie dogs and cellar doors and freezer ice cream and all kinds of things that had nothing to do with New York.

"You like it, I hope? You were crazy about it when we bought it."

"It looks very pretty." It did, but it was someone else's home, not mine. I remembered my home. It was in New York, in an East Side apartment. My home was there, with my children. I put the picture down on a table. "Dave. I want to go home. Please."

"Soon, darling, soon. Be patient."

His arms around me, his face close to mine. The smell of whiskey. Why did he always drink before he came to see me? I felt suddenly gay, as though I were drunk by osmosis. I pulled him toward the bed. "Come on. Hop into bed!"

"Honey, you know we can't."

"Why not? We're married."

"It's just not allowed."

"Oh, come on, they won't know."

"No, darling. It's not that I don't want to! Believe me, I miss you like anything."

"Well, then?" Again it seemed like a child's problem in arithmetic. I wanted to go to bed with him. He wanted to go to bed with me. Therefore, we should be allowed to go to bed! Why was he being so dull and stodgy?

"For another thing, you're not prepared."

"So what? We'll have another baby! Oh, wouldn't that be nice, honey? Another beautiful baby!"

"Mmmm. Don't you want me to tell you about the house?" He pulled an envelope and a pen from his pocket. "Here, I'll draw you a floor plan."

To please him, I allowed myself to be diverted.

Sometimes I went with a group of patients to another floor for what I suppose was called "occupational therapy." We sat around long wooden tables in a very large room and obediently worked on our projects.

The walls of the room were hung with watercolors and oil paintings done by the patients. I remember walking around the room one day, looking at them all carefully because I thought it would be interesting to see what kind of work mental patients would do. I expected scenes of violence and obvious sexual symbolism, but I was disappointed. The subjects were surprisingly ordinary: a vase of roses on a blue, fringed cloth; a still life of fruit in a bowl; a sunset with two trees in the foreground and three clouds that looked like mashed potatoes. Perhaps the therapist had told the patients what to paint.

She was a plump, middle-aged woman with large dark eyes and a lined face. She walked as though her feet hurt and always wore a smock printed with big red roses on a black background. She yawned quite often as she moved from table to table, and that too surprised me; I wondered whether she was tired or merely bored. I had always thought unshakable enthusiasm was a necessity for anyone working with the mentally ill. It rather pleased me to imagine that she was as bored as I was.

I was trimming the edges of a small leather wallet with leather stitching. The wallet itself was tan; the leather strips for the stitching were dark brown. Even had it been done well, the finished product would have been unattractive, I thought. As it was, my work was so sloppy that the task began to seem as useless as thumb-twiddling. Nevertheless, I stitched on, slowly and clumsily. It did not occur to me to ask the therapist for something else to work on. Now and then she stopped by to see my progress. "That's coming along just fine," she would say each time.

Sometimes I merely looked at her in scornful silence. Other times I said belligerently, "I think it looks terrible."

She ignored my scorn and disagreed with my belligerence: "No, no, you're doing fine."

I was always glad when the time was up and I could lay aside that foolish wallet and return to the more honest boredom of the dayroom, where at least there was no pretense that you were doing anything but waiting for time to pass.

From time to time someone would call out: "R.T." Then all the third-floor patients assembled by the locked door at the end of the corridor. After we had filed through the doorway, we waited, in a clump, while the door was locked behind us. Then we were herded into the elevator and conveyed to the top floor of the hospital, to the recreation room.

I suppose R.T. stood for recreational therapy. I never wondered about it. When I heard the announcement, I quickly combed my hair and powdered my nose and put on lipstick. We met with the male patients during R.T. time, and I automatically tried to look my best for them.

(I wonder now how I did look during that month in the hospital. I say that I combed my hair and powdered my nose and put on lipstick, but perhaps I am remember-

ing only one or two occasions when I did this. What
about all the other days? Did I wander around disheveled? It is not a pleasant thought. I don't believe that
I washed or set my hair while I was there. However, it is
possible that I did so and that I have forgotten. The other
day I said to David, "I must have looked terrible in the
hospital." He replied diplomatically, "Well, I've seen
you look better.")

The recreation room was a large, cheerful room with
an adjoining terrace. Out on the terrace we played ring
tennis or sat and sunned ourselves. Inside there was a
pool table and a Ping-pong table, and scattered through
the room were card tables with all sorts of games and
puzzles lying about on them. Both the pool table and
the Ping-pong table were popular with the patients, but
few of us had sufficient powers of concentration for the
puzzles. Most of us were too restless to settle down very
long at anything. We wandered around the room, picking up objects, putting them down again, like pre-
schoolers exploring a nursery. Squabbles were frequent; games were started, then abruptly broken off.

I remember very little of how I spent my R.T. hours.
I know I made a few attempts at Scrabble, but it seemed
to me then a difficult, highly intellectual game. On the
other hand, I found dominoes too simple.

I recall that one day I asked a young girl to play chess
with me, without even considering whether I still remembered how to play. She said that she didn't know
how to play but that she would like to learn. I set up the

pieces on the board and began explaining the moves to her. It seemed to me that my explanations were quite clear and orderly. She found them difficult to follow.

"No, no," I said. "The knight moves like this: always in an L. It can't move straight forward."

"You're a terrible teacher," she said.

"Well, you're a terrible pupil," I replied.

Did we ever finish the game? Who was she, anyway, and why was she in the hospital? Did I play chess with anyone else? I don't know. Later, when I was at home again, I found in my bag several small black and white plastic chess pieces. If they had been all the same color it might have made sense; they might have been trophies of the last game I had played in the hospital. But black *and* white pieces? Had I just scooped up a handful of pieces after I had finished playing? Or had I considered the pieces I won in a game mine forever, and gone on to the next game without them? My chess playing, which I had thought so masterful, must have been as mad as the Mad Hatter's tea party.

Toward the end of the month I had a few visitors. I would have been allowed to have them sooner, but David kept them away until in his judgment I was ready to receive them. Even then he allowed only three people outside the family to see me. He thought that once I was well, I would not enjoy knowing that I had been seen in a disoriented state.

I am glad that he did this, but while I was in the hospital I was delighted to see everyone who visited me. As far as I know, my only visitors were my sister Martha, who came with her husband, my sister Sara, who came alone, three women friends, and my psychiatrist.

David told me later about these visits, but I do not remember them. He said I was allowed to go for walks outside the hospital grounds with my visitors and that I sat on a park bench with them, when the weather was good, and sometimes stopped at newsstands to buy magazines, cigarettes, and candy. He also brought the children to visit me, because I had asked so often to see them. We met in the lobby of the hospital. I do not remember this meeting at all. His eyes were sad when he told me about it later. "It was terrible," he said. "You'd begged for days to see them, but when they got there, you were, well, so *remote,* so dazed. They crawled around on the floor and explored everything—the chairs, the plants, the people. And you just kind of sat there." I am glad the children were no older than they were: mere babies.

I suppose my visitors must have been apprehensive before seeing me. They must have wondered whether I would be depressed or hostile or irrational, and what in the world they should talk to me about. I would have in their place: I have never visited anyone in a mental hospital. I imagine you must worry about saying "the wrong thing."

What did we talk about during those visits? I have not the slightest idea. I remember that they all smiled a lot. It did not occur to me to be suspicious of all this cheerfulness, since I became maniacally cheerful whenever I had a visitor. I remember that they all asked "How *are* you?" with that special intonation people use when genuine concern rather than courtesy prompts the question.

"Fine! Fine!" I always replied, quite truthfully. I hadn't a worry in the world except boredom. I suppose that is what shock treatment does for you. It screened out all the unpleasant aspects of life, and I existed in a cozy, comfortable little world.

I felt no shame or embarrassment before my visitors. I complained to them of boredom and told them that I wanted to go home, but I did not expect them to be able to change my situation. I accepted it, as a child, beneath his complaints, accepts the inevitability of bedtime. I was in the hospital because I had been brought there. I would be released when "they" decided to release me. In the meantime, I laughed with my visitors, hugged them to me, pleaded with them to stay longer when the hour was up, thanked them profusely for the flowers and candies and books and magazines they brought, and forgot all about them almost as soon as the door had closed behind them.

After a month in the hospital and ten shock treatments, I was released. I had my last treatment on the morning of the day that I left. I don't remember packing my things or any of the formalities of leave-taking. My memory of that day begins at the moment when David and I stood on the sidewalk, before the entrance to the hospital.

He peered anxiously at me. "Shall we get a cab?"

I had no idea where the hospital was; no picture at all in my mind of our apartment or its location.

"How far is it to the apartment?"

"Only a few blocks."

"Let's walk then."

Hand in hand, like lovers, we walked. It was a beautiful day for July: sunny, yet almost cool, like those crisp days New York often has in early fall. The sun picked out mica in the stone of luxury apartment buildings: its glitter and the sharp shade of the sky caused me to blink, like someone emerging from a darkened room. I responded to the day but did not appreciate its rarity: I could not have told what month it was or even what year. I was happy because I was no longer confined. I looked around with the thoughtless delight of a child out for a ride in her stroller. It pleased me to see plane trees lining the streets and to hear the faint rustle of their leaves, set against the clatter of city sounds. It pleased me to see cars and taxis and Puerto Rican delivery boys and women with bouffant hairstyles walking their dogs and children riding shiny tricycles. With an interest as avid as any sight-seer I peered into elegant shop windows, many of which displayed signs saying CLOSED FOR THE SUMMER, and reviewed the rows of brownstones, freshly painted in pastel shades—pink, yellow, green, beige—well-kept houses with starched

toes and fingers, gently moved his fist from beneath his chin, studied his closed eyes, marveled at his film of fine blond hair. Then the nurse took him away and I floated in euphoria until he was returned to me, that time to nuzzle at my breasts.

And Elizabeth? I tried to remember going to the hospital to have my daughter, but I could not. What time of year was it? Summer, I thought. I wasn't sure. During the day or at night? I could not remember anything of her birth except the presence of that black patent leather hatbox in my hospital room. By then it was getting shabby. A piece of wire poked its way through the leather and tore the stocking of a nurse who carried it into my room. She kept after me about that stocking in a half-serious, half-teasing way. When I offered to buy her new stockings, she indignantly said no, yet she could not leave the subject alone.

I understand now, five years later, why I remember so little of my daughter's birth. Her birth was clouded by the news that my father was hopelessly ill with cancer. He had learned this shortly before he was to leave for a visit to his children. He should not have traveled, but he ignored his doctor's orders and came north anyway, suffering through the long train ride with his usual stoicism. A few days after he arrived at my sister Sara's, he suffered a severe hemorrhage, so the rest of the family —he had intended to keep it a secret—learned of his illness.

My baby was due in a few days, so I too was not supposed to travel, but David and I immediately took the train out to my sister's house: I felt that I had to see my father. When we arrived at the house, I was told that he was resting in his room. The door to his room was open. He was seated in a rocker, his eyes closed, a stone sculpture. "Daddy!" I said. He opened his eyes, smiled at me, and struggled to his feet, insisting that I take the rocker, the only comfortable chair in the room, because I was about to bear a child.

Back at home, awaiting my child, I was haunted by the fear that my father would die on the day that my child was born. At that time we had no idea that his disease would progress so slowly. We all thought that he would not last long. In the hospital, on the day that Elizabeth was born, as I lay in bed, relieved and happy that she was a healthy, normal baby, I dreaded answering the telephone, which rang often. I should not have clung to him so; it was not fair to my daughter.

But as I walked along the street with David, a year after Elizabeth's birth, I did not remember all that. I only knew that I was glad to be going home, glad to be free of the starch and bustle of nurses. I knew that I was leaving a hospital, but I did not know why I had been there. I believe I had asked David, but did not retain his answer for more than a few seconds. In any case, it didn't matter to me: I was too exhilarated by my new freedom to be concerned with what had happened and why.

At the entrance of our apartment building I stopped, abruptly anxious, and held Dave's hand back to keep him from opening the door. "Will the children remember me?" I did know that I had been away for quite some time.

"Of course," he said.

David always lies when he thinks that I want to hear a lie. He has no qualms about it. Later, if his lie is revealed as such, he does not apologize. I am not at all like him in this respect. Most of the time I am comforted by his lies or half-truths; sometimes they annoy me. On this occasion I was glad to hear his confident "Of course."

We took the elevator to our floor. He opened the door to our apartment. I entered, tensely prepared for the worst—blank stares from my two babies, perhaps even cries of fright—and found that the apartment was empty. Victoria, who had worked for me part-time before I went to the hospital and was now working full-time, at the insistence of Dr. Rosen, had taken the children to Central Park, apparently.

"That's good!" David said, pushing me toward the living room couch. "Sit! We'll celebrate alone."

He disappeared into the kitchen. I sat down on the couch and looked around the room. It looked both familiar and unfamiliar at the same time. It was rather like that sensation of *déjà vu* you sometimes have when you enter a strange room. Or rather, it was the reverse of *déjà vu*. Everything in the room was known to me, yet *seemed* strange. I had bought those scatter pillows at Bloomingdale's. I had ordered the chairs and end tables from Knoll's, through the friend of a friend who is a decorator, and waited forever for them to arrive. I had bought that hand-woven Indian rug from Sloane's and gone to Bonnier's for the lamps and to Takashimaya for the ashtrays. I *knew* that all of these things belonged to me, yet I couldn't be sure it wasn't some trick of the mind that made me "know" this, some psychological phenomenon I could find described in textbooks, listed under an impressive Latin name. I looked around the room like a guest who inspects the premises while her host is out of the room.

Perhaps the order of the room helped disorient me: it looked readied for guests. No ashes in the ashtrays, no toys or bottles lying around, no newspapers or magazines on the couches, no smudges or soot on the white tops of the end tables. No thread or crumbs or matches on the rug. Fresh philodendron leaves in the ceramic bowl on the dining room table. The smell of lemon oil. Every polishable surface gleaming.

David came in carrying a tray. Champagne. But of course. I might have known. He always believes in marking an occasion.

"Remember when you brought Larry home? You put him right there"—he motioned toward the end of the couch—"and then we drank champagne."

"Yes." He had lain there sleeping, cocooned in his receiving blanket, while David and I toasted him. How easy it is to take care of a baby, I thought then. Look! He just lies there and sleeps. But the second day he cried

endlessly, until finally, feeling bewildered and anxious
and tired, I too cried.

"Well—" David said, holding his glass toward mine.
"To you. Welcome home."

We touched our glasses, smiled at the ritualistic ring
of glass striking glass. "No—to us," I said.

We drank our champagne. We smiled at each other.
David turned on the phonograph, rummaged through
the records until he found Purcell's *The Fairy Queen*,
put it on after asking politely, "All right if I play some
records?" as though I were a guest rather than a wife.

I was a guest. I do not live in an immaculate apartment and drink champagne at eleven o'clock in the
morning. I sat passively while he moved about, changing records, pulling up the long split-bamboo shade to
let in more light, pouring champagne. We talked a little: So good to have you home. So good to *be* here. That
sort of thing.

I was relieved when we finished the split of champagne.
I hadn't had any alcohol in a month, and this had made
my face feel unpleasantly hot. I thought also that maybe
I would be allowed to stop smiling since there was no
more champagne.

The record came to an end. The arm lifted, swung
over, dropped down, and the phonograph shut itself
off. An eye of light on the carpet to warn you: the power
is still on, although the music is not. The whine of the
elevator. The clang of its doors opening, then closing
again. The children? Or the neighbors? A key turning in

the lock. The children! It was like that terrible moment
in a dream when you're confronted with danger, but you
can't run away; you're frozen until finally the intensity
of the agony wakes you up. I wanted to see my children,
I *had* to see them, yet I was terrified; their indifference
seemed a danger more dreadful than any nightmare.

From where I sat on the couch, I could see down the
hall to the front door of the apartment. The door opened.
My small son appeared.

"Mama!" A shrill, thrilling cry, like silk tearing.

Clumsy with excitement, he raced down the hall,
crashed once, twice into the wall. I jumped up, then
stooped down with arms outspread to receive his body
as he hurled himself into my arms. "Mama! Mama!
Mama!" He had to say it over and over, as though
I might vanish if not evoked. His shirttail was hanging
out; his hands and mouth were sticky; his blond hair,
bleached silvery by the sun, was too long. I tasted the
salt of his sweat as I kissed his hair; I covered him with
kisses, marveled at the softness of his cheek, the faint
smell of orange juice on his breath: my flesh, my blood,
with a breath of his own. Tears blurred my vision.

A few seconds later, I became aware of Victoria standing in the doorway, holding Elizabeth. My baby. Wrig-
gling, wild to break free of those encircling arms, wav-
ing her own plump baby arms, laughing her own deep,
delightful laugh. She knew me! She remembered! I had
forgotten her, but she remembered!

I untangled myself from Larry and opened my arms

to Beth. She cuddled to me, pliable as a rag doll, murmured sounds that were almost a song. When I blew into
her fine brown hair, she lifted her head from my breast,
giggled, then snuggled down again. I wished I could
nurse her; I longed for a breast full of milk; I wanted
to see her greedy mouth sucking at my nipple. I could
hardly remember when I did nurse her; so long ago, a
few weeks, then an infection in my breast. A sense of loss
mingled with the hope that David now might share the
middle-of-the-night feedings.

Still holding Beth, I sat down on the couch. Larry
followed me. He pulled at me, tried to find room on my
lap, pushed and poked and fingered me. "Mama home!
Mama home! Hold me! Hold me!" he said. I moved
Beth over and held them both.

"You see," David said. He had been standing in the
living room, watching me, a fond smile on his face. "You
always worry when there's no need to."

Victoria, a slight, beautiful Jamaican girl, standing
shyly in the doorway, said, with a lilt in her voice, "It's
good to have you home, Mrs. Wolfe."

Home. Yes, I was home. My hands were full again: I
was home.

But I no longer knew how to be a mother. The next
morning I woke up to the sound of both babies crying.
David was asleep—or was pretending to be still asleep.
I remembered that on Sundays when we had been out
late the night before, we used to feign sleep, each hop-

ing the other would get up to tend the children. In the end, I always did, but I never gave up thinking each week: Maybe this time he'll get up. I considered waking Dave and asking him to help me; it seemed years since I had actually done anything for the children. The day before, I had merely played with them. Victoria and David had done all the feeding and bathing and diaper changing. But I could not go on being an invalid forever. It was time I got back to work. I snuggled down under the covers for a few more seconds, and then, as the screaming of both children increased in volume, I reluctantly climbed out of bed and went down the hall to my son's room.

His screaming stopped when I opened the door. "Hi, Mama! More come in!"

His smile was generous. Clearly, he thought me the most wonderful sight in the world. At that moment, I felt the same extravagance of feeling for him. But down the hall, Beth continued to howl. How had I ever managed two babies at once? I leaned against the doorway, wondering what to do. Larry clambered about in his orange and gold crib, beaming at me. His blue flannel pajamas were soaked with urine. I couldn't get him up and let him run around like that. And I didn't want to have to listen to her screams while I changed and dressed him. If I left him to go and change her, then he would start crying again. Suddenly, one fragment of the morning routine returned to me: crackers. You throw them crackers and that shuts them up while you change them.

I hurried down the hall to the kitchen, grabbed a handful of crackers from a box still sitting on the table from the night before, opened Beth's door, stuck a cracker in each of her hands (she stopped crying immediately and began the serious business of eating), hurried back to Larry's room, gave him a cracker, lifted him out of his crib, hastily changed him and dressed him in a white knit shirt and brown knit pants while he chewed on his crackers, and led him down the hall to Beth's room. We got there just in time. Beth, having finished her crackers, was clutching the sides of the crib and shaking them in a fury of frustration. I sat Larry down on the floor with a blue plastic truck while I changed Beth and jammed her fat body into a pink stretch suit. Then I carried her into the kitchen and plopped her into the high chair, Larry following close on my heels.

So far, so good. I was feeling rather pleased with myself. Then, as Beth began to bang on the tray of her high chair and Larry climbed up on his chair shouting, "Lunchtime!" my pleasure vanished. I hadn't the slightest idea what to feed them for breakfast. It is easy enough now to think: Well, what did it matter what they had for breakfast that one morning? Anything would have done. But then I felt helpless, maimed. I looked at the clock in the hall. Ten after eight. What time was Victoria coming? I didn't know. Probably not until nine or nine thirty. Again I thought: Should I wake up David?

He hates getting up early. I had no idea what time we had gone to bed. I couldn't even remember how we had spent the evening.

"More lunch, Mama," Larry demanded.

From Beth, screams, because she saw Mama merely standing there. The kitchen seemed huge. There were cabinets everywhere: above the sink, the washing machine, and the butcher's block, and from floor to ceiling on the wall opposite the stove. Which one held whatever it was they ate for breakfast?

"More lunch, Mama!"

I ran down the hall to our bedroom and shook David to wake him up. "Dave! Dave! You have to get up! I don't know what to feed the children!"

He sat up immediately, frowning. "What time is it?"

"Ten after eight. Oh, please help me. I'm sorry, I know you hate to get up early . . ."

He managed to smile at me. "It's okay, hon. Be there in a second."

In a few minutes David joined me in the kitchen and showed me how to prepare breakfast for the children. I sat on a stool and watched intently as he moved about the room, testing the temperature of Beth's milk on his wrist, fastening plastic bibs around both children's necks, picking up Beth's spoon when she dropped it, getting juice for Larry when he demanded it.

"Tomorrow I'll do everything," I promised. "I just couldn't think what to give them."

"That's because of the shock treatment," he said, as

he was to say so many times in the weeks to come. "Your memory will come back. Just don't worry about it."

But the next morning was exactly the same. I managed to get them up and dressed and into the kitchen, but everything David had shown me the day before had vanished from my mind. Again I had to wake him up and ask him what the children had for breakfast. Again he got up and fixed it. And the next morning was the same. This time, however, he merely told me, as he lay in bed, "Warm milk, warm bottled fruit, powdered cereal for her; cold milk, dry cereal, fresh fruit for him," and I was able to do the preparation and feeding by myself.

"You see," David said, as we sat in the dining room drinking coffee while Victoria got the children ready for the park, "you're improving. This morning you fixed their breakfast. Maybe tomorrow you won't even have to ask what to give them."

I couldn't match his enthusiasm. It didn't seem like much of an accomplishment. "Three days in a row I have to ask what my children eat! It feels so weird!"

Again the same refrain: "It's not your fault. It's the shock treatment."

I didn't care whose fault it was. I only knew it was very difficult to try to function when so much of your memory had been taken from you. Fortunately, we could afford to have Victoria come in every day while I slowly reoriented myself. And during the evenings began what I called the "reconstruction period."

* * *

"Tell me what happened. I mean, how did I act before I went to the hospital?"

I was stretched out on the living room couch. The children were asleep. David was sitting in his favorite chair, the big orange one, smoking his pipe. It was three or four days since I had returned from the hospital. Perhaps I had asked him the same question before—once, or twice, or dozens of times. If so, I did not remember his answer. I do remember that on this occasion I was almost afraid to ask him, but I felt it was my duty to. I had to know, I had to face all the facts, no matter how unpleasant they might prove to be.

"You remember going to see your parents?"

Until he said it, I had not.

"Your father is dying. Do you remember that, dear?"

Again I felt as though I were awakening from a dream. But I did not want to wake up. I did not want to live in a world where people grew old and died. My father had cancer. Now I remembered.

Don't die, don't. You are eighty years old, but you can't die because my children need a father. I mean grandfather. Why did I say father when I meant grandfather? It is I who need a father, I suppose.

I never knew Daddy when he was young. He was always old—in his fifties when I was born. As long as I can remember, I thought: He's old. What if he dies? Please God, don't let him die. Every other month, when he went on the road, traveling from town to town, to all those little Southern towns I had never seen, I always thought he would never come back. We always knew where he was: we had his route sheet all neatly typed out. We kept it on the sideboard in the dining room, behind the silver pitcher, but I didn't know where he was; I only knew he was gone. I would go to bed and say my prayers: "Now I lay me down to sleep, I pray the Lord my soul to keep. If *he* dies before I wake, I pray the Lord my soul to take."

"Dear?"

David's voice. Not Daddy's. David's. I said, "I'm going to get some water. Want anything?"

"I could use a drink."

"Scotch or bourbon?"

"Bourbon."

I drank a glass of water in the kitchen and then went on back to the living room with David's drink. I stretched out on the couch again.

"Is that why I went home? Because he is dying?" I asked.

"Well, partially. You wanted to see him, of course. But the other thing was, I thought you needed to get away for a while. You kept saying how tired you were. You worried so much about the children. As it was, you didn't want to leave them. I practically insisted that you go —and your class was having a reunion . . ."

"How long did I stay with them?"

"Five days. You went to the hospital four days after you got back."

"But what did I do? How did I *act?*"

"Well, you came back all elated. You said you had a marvelous time. You kept talking and laughing and telling stories about things you'd done . . ."

As he spoke, I was beginning to remember what it had been like, being home again. In a way, it was rather like being a child again. I had left my husband and children behind. I was back with the friends of my girlhood, back in the lush, semitropical atmosphere I had known and loved as a child. Life in New York was black and white, a documentary; home was a Technicolor, Vistavision movie. I had left behind urine-soaked diapers, Pablum, Zweibach crumbs, the noise, dirt, hurry, and anger of New York. The sweet Southern voices that surrounded me were so familiar, so soothing. It was like swimming in the Gulf of Mexico: the salt in that tepid water buoys you, makes swimming seem effortless. The air was humid, heavy with the scent of flowers; the grass was a vivid green; gardens were a jumble of overgrowth. All the sights and sounds and smells: a feast of epiphanies. My father was dying, but I had felt strangely alive —younger, gayer . . .

"You brought back a lot of things," Dave said. He got up and went over to the bookcase, picked something up, and came back to sit beside me. He opened a leather-covered pipe case and took out a meerschaum pipe. The bowl was carved into a lion's head, with bared fangs.

"It's marvelous! Where did it come from?"

"Your father gave it to me. Don't you remember?"

"He never smoked a pipe like that!"

"No. You said a friend gave it to him years ago. He told you it was too good to use."

I sighed. How like my father, and my mother too. Once poor, they would always feel poor. Anything luxurious or expensive was too good for them. It was wrapped up, put away, saved for the children.

David brought out other things: my old copy of *Little Women,* a pair of gold Victorian brooches, an ostrich plume fan, a sketchbook of my grandmother's filled with dainty, ladylike sketches of the English countryside and realistic floral studies. Each time he handed me an object, he handed me a fragment of my visit home. I remembered that my mother kept pressing objects she had always treasured into my hands, almost as though she were dying instead of my father. Did she imagine that she would die when he did?

I remembered that we talked together, my father and I, for brief intervals many times during the five or six days of my visit. Or rather, he talked to me—I had difficulty in making myself heard, his deafness had grown so bad. He always sat in the same shabby rocker; I always sat in the same straight-backed dining room chair; he always held my left hand with his large, arthritic right hand.

My father's hands. I knew their touch so well! He had always liked to sit on the front porch on warm evenings. He would ask me to join him if I didn't have homework or other things to do. And always, when I sat with him, he would reach for my hand . . .

One afternoon during my visit home, he gripped my hand with an unusual strength and said, "I want to tell you that you have never in your life done anything to cause me unhappiness. You are a fine woman and I have always been proud of you. *Always*."

I hadn't thought of my confirmation for years. Why did I think of it then? Because my father seemed to be granting me absolution? "Laying on of hands," the confirmation service is called. The bishop had placed his hand on my head, said a brief prayer, then moved on to the child kneeling beside me. The communion wine was heavy and sweet. I am drinking blood, I thought, and shivered with girlish delight.

"Thank you," I told my father. "I'm proud of you also."

I remembered too that each time he lay on the living room couch to rest (he could not sit up and talk to anyone for more than a half hour or so), I would think, as I looked at his closed eyes, his still body, his lax mouth and sunken cheeks: He's dead! I would calm myself by thinking: If he is, there isn't anything that I can do about it. Then in a few minutes he would stir, and I would know that he was alive, for the moment at least. Mother had hardly left his side for months. He could not go out; she would not leave him in the care of others. She fluttered about the house, in an exhausted frenzy. A sad, horrible, human situation.

"I can't imagine why I was *elated* when I came back," I said.

"You were pleased that your father's spirits were so

good. And that he was still keeping up with politics and the stock market. And your mother—you said you'd never realized how much strength she had. You got along well with her, better than you ever had—and you saw friends . . ."

"So if I was so happy, how did I end up in the hospital?"

David had put away all my childish things, my books and mementos, and returned to his chair, with another drink. He knocked the ashes from his pipe, filled it, and lighted it with agonizing deliberateness.

"You kept talking—you couldn't stop. You couldn't sleep. You were keeping me up all night talking. I'd beg you to let me go to sleep, but you'd laugh and say, 'Oh, don't be such a stick-in-the-mud!' And drinking! You drank bourbon all night long, iced tea glasses of it, and jumped around and played the radio, but all you wanted to listen to was rock 'n' roll."

I had done all this? Most of the time I am rather on the quiet side, if anything, pleasant but reserved. My taste in music is for Bach rather than the Beatles. I do not drink excessively.

"Why was I drinking so much?"

"Because you couldn't sleep. You took sleeping pills, but they didn't do any good, so you tried having a nightcap, and that didn't do any good, so you would have another and another. I didn't really get worried about you until I woke up at five o'clock one morning and you were on the phone. I'd fallen asleep from sheer exhaustion—even though you were crashing around the house, turning on all the lights and playing records. When I woke up you were talking to Miss Harding from your old office—you were insisting that she was related to you—on your mother's side. You said you knew she was a Davis."

"Oh, Dave!" I covered my face with my hands and lay on the couch without moving. In the hospital, when the nurse told me that I had had a breakdown, I did not feel any emotion at all. I wondered at the news with the kind of curiosity you feel when confronting a puzzle or a riddle. And since coming home, I had been occupied with trying to reorient myself into my surroundings. Now, for the first time since my breakdown, I felt shame. This, I suppose, was a giant step toward normality: to once again accept the responsibility for my actions. I was engulfed by shame. To call Miss Harding at five in the morning! Why, I must have been crazy! And if I was crazy four weeks ago, why should I assume I was sane now? I knew, as I lay there, that of course I was not related to her, but I felt also that I was no longer the person I had once been, because now I was a woman who had once been crazy enough to have this delusion.

Miss Harding. Elegant, aging, beautiful. Intelligent and witty. The antithesis of my mother, who is warm and dowdy and rambling. Miss Harding held a position of importance in the advertising agency for which I had once worked. My mother had never had a job. It was

easy enough to see why I, who have strong personal am-
bitions, should seek to relate myself to Miss Harding.
Yet I had never been conscious of feeling envy for her,
only awe. True, she lived in a large, antique-filled apartment, but she had neither husband nor children, and I
have both. I had often thought of asking her over, but I
had always felt that my home was not elegant enough,
or clean enough, even, for *her*. She was always immaculate, in clothes made to order, usually of silk. I thought
of her as always rustling faintly as she walked. Her bags
and shoes were Italian-made, of the softest, finest leather.
In the summer she used a sandalwood fan. Its sweet,
powdery scent surrounded her on the hot muggy days
that caused the rest of us to wilt. She did not seem real.
I thought that, like some beautifully made, elaborately
dressed mechanical doll, she must have within her an
intricate collection of gold wheels and wires that cause
her to talk and walk, stand and sit, as required. This was
the woman I had called at five in the morning!

"What did you do?" I asked David.

"I grabbed the phone away from you and apologized
to her and told her you had been upset lately and tum-
bled back into bed."

"And—"

"The next thing I knew you were on the phone again,
talking to Joan. You were telling her *she* was your
cousin. It was six o'clock this time."

"Oh, God!" I wasn't sure I wanted to hear any more,

but I knew I had to listen to whatever David would tell me. This too was unpleasant to hear, but at least Joan was a good friend.

I had known Joan then for more than ten years. I was hired by an advertising agency to succeed to her job. She stayed on at the agency for a few more months, and during that time we became close. David and I had a floor-through in the village then, and Joan and her husband, Rodney, who, like David, was a photographer, lived around the corner. We spent a lot of evenings with them, talking about our work, arguing over the merits of artists who had "made it," comparing boyhoods in New York and the Midwest, girlhoods in the South (Joan had also grown up in the Deep South).

David took to Rodney immediately, and liked and admired Joan, but he was puzzled a bit by my closeness to Joan. We were so different, he said, and it was true. Joan is short, overweight, with a round, childlike face and dark brown hair she wears cropped. My women friends have tended to be taller, more slender: mirror images of myself. And we are unlike in character, personality—call it what you will. Joan is ruthlessly ambitious, conditioned to that way of life by a mother who pushed her onto the stage at the age of three, poked and prodded her through classes in piano, dancing, singing, acting, all within a proper, Southern, social frame of reference. My mother had no ambition at all for me other than to get me married to a respectable man. Somehow I developed some aspirations on my own, but they never equaled Joan's.

Unlike though we were, Joan and I had much in common. Within that slick, rich advertising agency, Joan and I turned to each other for solace. We were not used to the coldness and rudeness of Northerners, even though we often made fun of the silly manners of Southerners. However, we grew somewhat apart after I had my children. We moved uptown; they still lived in the Village. She and Rodney had no children, so, necessarily, our daily lives differed. She was able to lie in bed all morning, to work all night at her writing with a feverish intensity, chewing up pencils, smoking too much, drinking too much bourbon, pushing her fingers into her bangs until they stuck up like quills. I, however, had to get up at six to look after my children, had a husband who expected to come home to a clean apartment and a good dinner. If there was no time left for my writing, who cared? Only I did, and sometimes I envied Joan her freedom, her self-indulgence. It wasn't difficult to understand why I had chosen to relate myself to Joan.

"I finally got you to bed," David said. "You had an appointment with Dr. Stern that morning."

"Why was I going to see him if I was so happy?"

"You were happy most of the time—but all of a sudden you'd start to cry. So you called him a couple of days after you got back. You went over there that morning and he phoned me. 'Why haven't you called me?' he said. 'She's in bad shape. I don't understand why you didn't call me.' He sounded very upset. And you can imagine how I felt."

I listened as he spoke, but his words awakened no memories.

"Do you remember any of that now?"

"No. But go on."

"He said he was sending you to another doctor who specialized in cases like yours. You went there alone in a cab and then Dr. Rosen called me. He said, 'Your wife has to go to the hospital right away.'

"I thought you wouldn't want to go. But he said, 'Don't worry about that. I'll get her there. I'll tell her she needs a rest.'

"I had to rush home and pack some things for you— he told me what you'd need—three dresses were all you were allowed to have—and I met you at the hospital—"

"Did I mind? I mean, didn't I object to being put in the hospital?"

"Oh, darling, you were so *tired!* You hadn't really slept since you got back. But you wanted a private room. When I said we couldn't afford one, you said, 'But I always have a private room!'

"I told Dr. Rosen, 'She wants a private room. But I can't afford it—not for a whole month.' He said, 'Don't let it worry you. She won't even remember what kind of room she had.' As it was, the whole business cost over three thousand dollars."

Three thousand dollars! *Our* money, but because he had earned it, I always felt it was his, really. Three thousand dollars spent in a month because I had cracked up. If I had had a tumor or cancer or any other physical ailment, I would have thought: Well, it isn't my fault. But a nervous breakdown clearly *was* my fault.

David came over and sat beside me. "I don't want you even to think about the money. It's spent and you're well and that's that."

Of course he wanted me to think about the money. Otherwise, he would not have mentioned it. Like most men who do not have a steady salary or a predictable income, David worries about money. Actually, he is well established in his profession, as he deserves to be, for he is a highly talented man. One wall of his studio is almost covered with awards he has won, ranging from "gold medals" to "certificates of excellence." And he has always made enough to support his family comfortably; but I have never known a free-lance photographer or illustrator who did not worry, who did not have fantasies that some day the telephone would stop ringing, that some day there would simply be no more assignments.

Every three months David's accountant goes over his books, and every time he says, "Dave, you're spending too much money." Then for the next few days David storms around the house looking for signs of waste. He switches off lights or demands to know why I have bought a loaf of bread at the delicatessen instead of at the supermarket. But soon he is back to normal again: not extravagant, but not worrisome, either, about money; fond of occasional luxuries, such as wine and flowers and theater tickets and taxis. With my illness and the buying of the house coinciding, financial burdens had increased suddenly, unexpectedly—and it was all my fault.

"I'm sorry it cost so much," I said in a small voice. (Love me, love me, please love me, even though I am weak and crack up and you are strong.)

"Don't talk like that. It's not your fault."

His words were comforting, but it *was* my fault. I knew it. He knew it too. You can't blame your breakdown on someone else; it's *yours*. In the past, when I grew depressed he would say, "If you would only put your mind to it, you could stop being depressed." He made it sound so easy. But it was not easy.

"Do you know what that Dr. Rosen of yours did?" David asked. "He may be a good doctor, but he's a bastard."

"Why? What do you mean?" Roused from self-pity, I was interested. I was to go see Dr. Rosen the next day. My memories of him were: brown eyes, a Harvard accent, a brown and white checked suit, an aura of kindness.

"He handed me a bill in the *admitting room!* Can you imagine that! I'm frantic with worry—I'm sitting there answering all the questions—you're not even in your room yet—he hands me a piece of paper and I take it and I think maybe it's something else I have to sign and it's a *bill!* How could anyone with any feelings hand you a bill at a moment like that?"

Money again. Poor Dave, I thought. I'll make it up to you some day. A childish thought. I'm sorry I broke your vase, Mama. When I grow up, I'll get rich and buy you another. Crazy talk. I can't grow up. I'll never get rich. I'll never make it up to you.

"I'm sorry," I said.

"Don't ever say that. Promise me you won't ever say that or even think it."

"All right."

"Don't you think we ought to be going to bed now?"

"I want to lie here for a while," I said. "You go on."

I felt like a shopper who has so many bundles she does not know how to manage them. They were all sizes and shapes, clumsily wrapped, about to burst open. I was approaching a revolving door. I had somehow to get through it carrying all my bundles. Perhaps I should put some down, carry the most important through, then return for the others. My father is dying—surely that is the most important. But I did not want to think about that. Put that down, forget about it, return for it later, when you are stronger. Think, instead, about the odd things you did. Try to remember calling Miss Harding and Joan.

I could not. I wondered why it seemed so important to me to remember. I seemed to feel that if I did not recall those memories, bring them up to the light and air of the surface, they would fester in my mind and spread their virulence. But straining to remember never helps. It only causes the memory to submerge even deeper. I realized that I was tired, so I got up, straightened the pillows, emptied the ashtrays, carried Dave's glass back to the kitchen, and went to bed.

I was tired, but I did not fall asleep for a long while. In the bed beside mine, David snored. I reached out and jabbed at him until he rolled over; his snoring ceased.

I was tired and I wanted to sleep; I had to get up early in the morning and prepare myself for my appointment with Dr. Rosen. It seemed to me that I had to look my best; wasn't there just the merest chance that he might say back to the hospital with you, dear, if anything were askew? Like an anxious student reviewing before an exam, I lay in bed and ticked off what I had decided to wear. (For what if I were to forget, as I forgot so many things, and in the morning, wander about the house without the slightest idea of what to put on?) The red linen dress. It's clean—and more important, it doesn't look at all depressed. The black patent leather pumps, my only shoes with heels that passed inspection. The black straw bag; it was lying on the chest of drawers where it was sure to be seen, could not be forgotten while I dressed. Black and white striped cotton gloves, drying in the bathroom. Two black bamboo bracelets. I had even thought to lay out two tiny safety pins on the bathroom shelf: I would need them to hold my lingerie straps in place. (If I look impeccable, perhaps he will not realize that my mind is as sloppy as my closet.)

David stirred, began to snore again. In their rooms my two babies slept. I heard faint traffic noises from the street; the screech of brakes, the slam of a car door, an engine starting up. The room was dark. I could barely make out the lump that was my husband lying in his bed.

I have had a nervous breakdown. This was now the central fact of my existence.

When you buy a new pair of shoes, the shoes, no matter how well made or properly fitted, feel strange to your feet. In the store you walk up and down on the soft carpets shoe stores always have. You study your feet in a mirror. You curl your toes up and down to flex the shoes, and finally you say, "Well, all right, I'll take them." At home, in your bedroom, you try your new shoes on again. Again you walk up and down, to break in your new shoes, to get used to them.

I have had a nervous breakdown. This fact was like a pair of ugly, stiff black oxfords. I had not bought them. Someone else had forced me into them.

I had to keep thinking it over and over; I had to keep trying it on: I have had a nervous breakdown.

I did not like my ugly new shoes.

If the shoe fits, wear it.

But it doesn't fit! I'm not crazy! Crazy people crack up, have breakdowns. I'm just neurotic.

Joan's psychiatrist said to her when she complained

that she wasn't getting any better, "Well, you've never been hospitalized."

I have been.

David used to say: "You have nothing to be depressed about. You have everything. A husband who loves you. Two lovely children. A nice apartment. You're pretty and bright and healthy."

Now I do have something to be depressed about: I have had a nervous breakdown.

David is asleep. I wish he would wake up. I want him to smile at me and say, "Darling, you're fine."

Am I?

He says the doctor says I'm going to be all right.

Am I?

Or am I mad? Temporarily sane now, but basically mad?

In the morning I put on my brave red dress and lipstick that matched it exactly, but I did not feel at all brave as I set forth to see Dr. Rosen. I did not trust myself to remember his address; I wrote it on the back of an envelope and tucked the envelope into the side pocket of my handbag.

David had told me that his office was just off Lexington, so I walked over to Lexington to take the bus downtown. I could not remember where the bus stopped. I asked a woman who was pushing a stroller (hoping she was not someone who had seen me often in the neighborhood), and I walked up to the corner she had indicated. A bus was coming. I opened my bag to get out the fare and realized that I was not even sure what it was. I *thought* the fare was fifteen cents; I was almost sure of it. But I was no longer a person who could be sure of anything.

I handed the driver a quarter. He handed me five nickels. I dropped three into the coinbox and waited to see his reaction. Just for a second, he shifted his attention from the traffic to give me a curious look, but he said nothing.

I moved away quickly, still clutching the remaining two nickels. I had forgotten that my father was dying of cancer. I had forgotten that we were buying a house in the country. I had forgotten that I had a daughter named Elizabeth, but at least I had remembered something: the bus fare in New York City was fifteen cents.

The doctor's building was one of those huge, enormously expensive co-op apartment buildings that have been appearing all over the East Side at a bewildering rate. (Are there really enough rich people around to fill them?)

The doorman, a small man with discouraged shoulders and a trace of an Irish accent, asked if he could help me.

"Dr. Rosen's office?" I asked, wondering if he had seen me being carted off to the hospital. Was he thinking: Ah, sure, she's one of the loony ones?

If he was, he did not show it. Matter-of-factly, he directed me toward one of the self-service elevators.

I rode up to the doctor's floor and rang his bell and waited.

Nothing happened. I didn't hear a sound. The hallway was long and narrow and carpeted and empty. Where was everyone this morning? No life spilled out from behind all those closed doors. No children howled, no dogs barked. I could not even hear a radio or a TV set. All was clean and sane and sanitary. I stood before the closed door and my palms began to sweat and I thought: You can't even go to the doctor's and get it right. It's the wrong place or the wrong day or the wrong time.

I didn't know what to do.

Dr. Stern has a sign on his door. RING BELL, WALK IN, the sign says.

Maybe I should try the door.

I turned the handle. The door opened.

I stepped into a small foyer furnished with two dainty little gilded chairs that seemed more for show than for sitting.

Beyond the foyer was a large room. Everything in it was gold and green and garish and glittering. *I am rich!* the room shouted. *Look at all the things I own.* Nothing was lean or spare or simple or worn. The carpet was thick. The cushions were fat. The arms of the chairs curved. Ornaments cluttered the tabletops. Velvet draperies, roped in gold, hung heavily at the expanse of windows.

I sat down on a couch. I was surprised to see that it was covered with a heavy plastic cover that showed, but sealed in, the velvet upholstery beneath it. Now, looking around, I saw that all the chairs had the same kind of plastic cover. (*I am rich, yes, but I am also careful with my possessions.*)

I felt quite superior, sitting there on that couch, because I would never cover furniture with plastic. Nevertheless, I sat stiffly. It was not a room you could relax in. Still feeling superior, I decided that he probably buys books by the yard. It's a wonder he doesn't have signs around saying: DON'T TOUCH ANYTHING!

In the foyer a door adjacent to the front door opened. I looked up. A man in a brown and white checked suit, an angry man, glared at me.

"Why are you sitting in the living room?" he demanded.

I fumbled for an answer. My mind was as clumsy as my hands. My hands couldn't seem to get a grip on my bag. It slid around on that plastic cover as though on a sheet of ice.

He didn't care how rational my answer might be. He didn't wait for it. He was outraged. "I purposely put those chairs here"—he gestured toward the small gilded chairs in the foyer—"and *still* you go and sit in the living room!"

Gloves in one hand, handbag secure in the other hand, I approached him. I had found the answer to his question: it did not deserve one. For his fury was like his furnishings: overdone, in questionable taste. The way to deal with such gaucherie was to ignore it or glance at it only obliquely.

"I didn't *hurt* anything," I murmured. I hoped the unspoken reference to his plastic covers reached him: You've taken care of that contingency, I meant to imply. You and your plastic couch covers. How *could* I hurt anything, even if I wanted to?

"Well, come in," he said. He managed a smile as he led me into the room that served as his office.

It was got up like a study rather than a doctor's office. One wall was lined with books: big, thick books that stood importantly on the shelves. His desk was dark, massive, heavily carved. Behind it two glass panels, here and there shot with colors as bright as Jello, shielded the windows. He had a couch, of course, but who would ever want to weep upon a couch covered with stripes of pink and green and gold? The wall above the couch was papered with diplomas.

I sat down in a pink chair that matched the couch. He sat down behind his desk. Who was your decorator? I almost asked. I wanted to be mean, to pay him back for shouting at me, but I realized that I would have to think of some more obvious way. For he would probably take the question for a compliment.

He watched me as I openly stared at his office. I suppose he expected me to say how nice it was. I said nothing and hoped that he was disappointed.

Finally he turned to the business at hand: "How are you feeling?"

I thought for a moment. What had I to say to a man who would scold you for sitting on his living room couch?

But after all, he was a doctor, and I was paying him. I ought to say something. "I had trouble sleeping last night," I said.

"I'll give you a prescription," he said. He jumped up, took down a thick book, and looked through it until he found the page that he wanted. Then he sat down and wrote out the prescription, using a fountain pen banded with gold.

When he handed me the prescription, I glanced at it to see how many pills he had prescribed. Thirty Nardols, then a few illegible squiggles, his name, followed by a frieze of degrees.

I folded the paper, tucked it into my wallet, and waited. "Anything else?"

He had scolded me. I did not want to talk to him. For a while I just looked at him. Despite his wall of degrees and the lines in his forehead and around his eyes, he still had a boyish look, the kind of look I used to call "cute" when I was a girl. I bet you were fast, I thought, and a good dancer. I bet you had a way of teasing girls that sent them spinning. I bet you had a convertible and drove it too fast.

Suddenly I remembered a boy I had known in college who had had a white Lincoln convertible. He was reported to be fabulously wealthy, an oil heir. He sat behind me in American history class and pulled my hair. When I turned around, he would assume a look of exaggerated innocence. I would have given anything to go out with him and go riding around in that white Lincoln convertible, but he never asked me. Eventually he married a girl who was Sweetheart of Sigma Chi in my junior year. He had to, it was rumored.

"Isn't there something you would like to talk about?"

Who is this man? Where am I? A split second before my mind snapped back to the present. Say something. You're supposed to talk. "I felt depressed yesterday. About having a breakdown."

"I'll give you something for that, too." Again he jumped up, took down his thick book, consulted it, then wrote out a prescription.

I let the minutes tick by. It was like sitting in an expensive bar, letting the ice melt in your drink just to show you were not really a drinker. I wanted to talk to him, I wanted to say: What happened? I don't understand. But I could not talk to him.

"Anything else?"

"Well—this house we're buying. It costs too much."

"Too much for what?"

"Well, just too much."

"What sort of house do you think you should be living in?"

"A house that costs thirty thousand dollars," I said promptly.

"Why thirty thousand dollars? Do you have any reason for picking that particular figure?"

"No. It just sounds better. More modest."

"If your husband can afford it, why shouldn't you live in a more expensive house?"

"Do you think I'll ever have to go back to the hospital?"

"Is that what you're worried about? That you might need the money for medical care?"

"No. I just got tired of talking about the house. I mean, I'm supposed to talk about whatever I want to, isn't that right?"

"Yes, of course."

Another long pause. Broken at last by him: "When is Dr. Stern coming back from his vacation?"

"The first of the month." How had I managed to remember that? I wondered.

"I'd like to see you three times a week until then."

Three times a week—to talk about what? I could not undress myself before a man who was so wrapped up in his possessions.

He jumped up again and brought a portable typewriter over to his desk.

I watched him while he typed. Finally I said, "Is that my case history or are you writing a novel in your spare time?"

He looked up and smiled at me. Then he yanked the paper from the typewriter and held it toward me. "It's your bill."

I glanced at it. It was typed in pseudoscript rather than ordinary typewriter letters. I studied it the way a child who cannot read studies a printed page. "What pretty type," I said. Then I grew up again: I read the bill. One office consultation—$35.

I looked at my watch. Ten fifteen. Too late to call, I decided. I'd call in the morning.

"Give me his number," I demanded when David returned.

He searched through his wallet and eventually found Dr. Stern's card.

When I took it from him, my hand trembled slightly. My whole self, body and mind, quickened at the sight of that familiar card. In print, his name, his address, his telephone number. Then: ADULT AND CHILD PSYCHIATRY BY APPOINTMENT ONLY. In his own handwriting, an area code, then the number of his summer home.

His own handwriting. Bold, masculine, written with a thick-nibbed fountain pen.

"Where are you going?"

"To my desk. I might forget to call tomorrow if I don't write it down on my calendar."

That was true—but more important, I think I wanted to be alone for a while. I sat at my desk and studied the card for a long time before I put it away.

In the morning, I realized that there had been no need for me to write down in my book: *Call Dr. Stern*. It was my first thought on awakening, superimposed over the howls of two hungry babies.

I was exceedingly patient with the children as I changed and dressed and fed them. So what if Beth threw the cereal I had so carefully prepared onto the kitchen floor? Hadn't I something important to do when the chores were done? The prospect of talking to Dr. Stern floated before me as I mopped the floor with a sponge and wiped sticky hands and chins and smeared Desitin onto a plump behind and dumped wet diapers into a pail.

When Victoria came in at nine, it still seemed too early to call. Ten o'clock, I decided, was the earliest possible time to call someone on a vacation. From nine to ten I merely waited for time to pass. Fool! I told myself. What do you expect from this telephone call?

"Hello," he will say.

And I will say, "Hello."

And like an umbilical cord, the telephone wire will connect us.

My hand crawled toward the telephone.

I moved it away. Too early. He is on his vacation. You must not be unreasonable.

But I have had a breakdown. There was nothing reasonable about it.

It doesn't matter. You must wait.

I made the beds. Nine fifteen. I wandered back to the kitchen and had another cup of coffee. Nine twenty. I played with Beth while Victoria put Larry's shoes on him. Nine thirty.

I said good-bye to the children. I washed the breakfast dishes. I went to the front door to see if the mail had come. It hadn't. I combed my hair and put on more lipstick. I sat down and stared at the living room rug. I thought I heard the super outside, so I went to the door again to see if the mail had come. It hadn't. I telephoned

"Time" to see if my watch were right. It was nine fifty-five.

I went to the bedroom, closed the door, sat down at my desk, and with a trembling finger dialed the number. (Fool! What do you expect? There will be an exchange of words. Nothing more.)

"Hello."

A child's voice—probably his son.

"Is Dr. Stern there?"

"He's out on the lake now."

Already remote from me, he grew more so. Out on the lake. Sailing, of course, the boy meant. I vaguely remembered that Dr. Stern was fond of sailing.

"When will he be back?"

"In about an hour."

"Will you please have him call this number?"

He listened, then repeated the number after me.

And I returned to my waiting.

When his call did come, it was, of course, an anticlimax.

We exchanged hellos. I told him how I was feeling (fine, thank you). I thanked him for the note he had written me upon my return home and apologized for calling him on his vacation, and he said that was quite all right, and I told him the reason for my call, and he said why don't you suggest to Dr. Rosen that you see him only once a week unless you feel you *need* to see him more? I said no, no, I don't need him. In a little girl's voice I said: I need you.

And he said, just as I say to my two-year-old, I'll be back soon. And he said call me at my office on the first and here before that if you need to. What happened to me? I said, still in a little girl's voice. And he said we'll talk about it when I get back. And I said I hope you're enjoying your vacation. And he said, oh, about as much as I ever do.

Good-bye.

Good-bye.

An exchange of words. Humdrum words. Ho-hum words.

I love you, Dr. Stern.

Why didn't I say that during our conversation?

"I'm not *in* love with you, but I love you. Transference, it's called. I dislike technical terms. I prefer to call it love.

I love you because you lean back in your chair and you listen when I say, "But it's so awful! To want to be a good person, someone who contributes to society, and instead to be petty and obsessed with money and trivia."

You say, "Why are you so hard on yourself?"

You smile at me and call me dear, and on the way to the door you quickly tell me about a movie you've seen or a book you've read, because I am not only your patient, I am also your friend.

I sat at my desk, my hand lingering on the telephone, and thought about our conversation and thought about the years spent seeing him sometimes twice a week, sometimes only once, year after year after year, and gradually I began to feel, not love for him, but resentment. It was like that shift in mood that sometimes occurs when I am drinking martinis with David.

After two drinks, I am alive with love. I call him darling and smile tenderly at him and am likely to reminisce about the early days of our marriage, when we lived in Greenwich Village. I no longer seek the wrinkles around his eyes or the stains on the living room carpet or the worn spots on the upholstery or the bald spot on the top of David's head.

Then gradually the glow which has surrounded me disperses. I am irritable and old. The living room simply must be redone. It is late and I have a million things to do and why have we frittered away so much time drinking? Dinner must be ruined! I bustle about, empty ashtrays, turn on lights, bang dishes around in the kitchen. David, who knows that food will restore my equilibrium, wisely disappears until dinner is on the table.

I wanted to call Dr. Stern back and say: No, I am not fine at all. Please explain to me why, after seven years of psychiatric treatment, I should have a nervous breakdown. I have paid you well over ten thousand dollars in fees, yet I had a breakdown, which cost three thousand more. Is psychiatry a fraud or is it merely you who are a fraud?

I did not call him, however. My resentment subsided. My equilibrium returned. Let him have his vacation in peace, I thought. He had tried to help me. He could not be blamed for his mediocrity any more than I could be blamed for mine.

I sat in a chair, facing Dr. Rosen, who was seated behind his desk. I wondered where to begin. I had to tell him that I did not want to pay him thirty-five dollars a visit and I felt that I had better get right to the point before too many thirty-five-dollar-an-hour minutes passed: he might want to throw me out when he heard what I had to say.

He was all smiles. His manner seemed social rather than therapeutic.

"What's so funny? What are you smiling about?" I said.

He leaned back in his chair and regarded me complacently. "I'm happy because you look so much better."

"Well, I'm not," I said flatly. So there. You needn't think you're so smart. "Listen. I can't afford to pay thirty-five dollars a visit. I can't come three times a week. We have so many expenses—with the house we're buying, and David's work isn't going well."

"Why isn't it?"

"He just isn't getting much work. That's the way it is when you free-lance. Sometimes you're busy and sometimes you're not, and when he isn't he worries all the time. He's been slow for months, and I just don't see how I can ask him for a hundred and five dollars a week."

He stared at the wall beside his desk. His eyebrows almost met in a frown.

"What are you thinking about?" I asked, borrowing a line from him. His smile had disappeared. Was I to be banished now?

"I was wondering why your husband's work should fall off at a time when the country's in a period of economic growth."

I had no time—at thirty-five dollars an hour—for any discussion of the American economy. "I don't know. I never paid Dr. Stern more than twenty dollars an hour."

He swung forward in his chair and faced me, hands folded on the desk before him. "Shall we say twenty-five dollars?"

"I can only come once a week," I warned.

"All right," he said pleasantly.

It was like yanking hard at a desk drawer you think is stuck, only to have it come tumbling out at once: the ease of the maneuver throws you off balance.

Silence. He leaned back in his chair. It creaked.

"How are you feeling? Are you taking the Equanil?"

"Yes."

"Does it help?"

"I don't know. Since I don't know how I would feel without it, how can I say whether it helps or not? I mean, I can't on any given day both *have* taken it and *not* have taken it, so as to compare. Why are you smiling?"

"You're very logical."

"Since when is logic amusing?"

"I told you, it's because I'm glad to see you so much better."

I slid my tortoiseshell bracelet up and down on my wrist; it clattered against the narrow gold bracelet David had given me for my birthday one year. My wedding ring, although gold, had left a mark like a bruise on my little finger. Too much iron in your blood, a jeweler once told me. I should have said there isn't enough. "Was I raving, then, before?"

Again that smile. He swung forward and picked up a brass letter opener. With its tip he tapped on the desk. "Well, you had some pretty bizarre notions."

"Bizarre notions?" David had told me that I talked quite sensibly in the hospital—except that I had forgotten a lot of things. He had lied! A hundred lurid possibilities occurred to me: I saw myself with disheveled hair, grabbing the arm of an aide, insisting I was Helen of Troy or Cleopatra or the Queen of Sheba. I did not want to think anymore. I did not want to know. Let sleeping dogs lie, my father used to say. A cliché. More comfortable, however, than this bloodletting they call psychiatry.

"Well, just a few," he qualified.

Was that supposed to comfort me? "For instance?" I couldn't stop myself from saying it.

"You thought Dr. Stern was in love with you." The lifted eyebrow, the half-smile, the eyes intently focused on my face: he was flirting with me. Was this supposed to be good psychiatric technique?

"Oh, well." I waved away the notion with my left hand; my bracelets banged together. "That's not so bizarre. Perhaps he is in love with me." I smiled so that he would know I was not serious. "Don't you think I'm lovable?" (Why was I preening when I wanted to weep? In the hospital this man had charged me with electrical currents. Here, too, the room seemed crazed with electricity. I could not go limp enough to weep.)

"Yes, I certainly do. But that doesn't mean that either Dr. Stern or I is in love with you."

"I know that," I said. I was annoyed that he had failed to see that I was joking. To change the subject, I said, "I talked to him yesterday."

"What did you talk about?"

"I told him you wanted to see me three times a week and I couldn't afford it. He was the one who said why didn't I just come once."

"Anything else?"

"I think I told him I was depressed."

"Is there anything in particular that you are depressed about now?"

"Yes. I thought now that I was home, I wouldn't keep forgetting things—I mean, things that happened after I left the hospital. But I do—and it upsets me. I see people, and then the next day I don't even remember that I've seen them."

"That will still happen for a while. But your day-to-day memory is getting better."

Day-to-day memory. A new concept. I turned it over in my mind as though it were a seashell I had found on the beach.

"And what about all the rest? What happened before I went to the hospital? I still don't remember any of that."

"It's not important that you do. Forget about the past. Put your thoughts on the future where they belong. When are you moving?"

"Oh, soon—I don't know exactly. The fifteenth, I guess." Forget about the past? We *are* the past. "I am a part of all that I have met," Tennyson said. I share his feeling: all that I have met is a part of me. I want it all. I don't want to give any of it up, any more than I want to lose an arm or a leg, or a child, born or unborn.

"That's very soon."

"Is it? I have trouble remembering the date. And even the year. The other day I was writing a check for Victoria, and I got to the date and I didn't know it, so I asked her, and she told me, but of course she didn't say the year. You're supposed to know that if you're walking around loose. So I wrote 1964, hoping it was right."

"I don't think you ought to move that soon. I think you ought to postpone it a month."

"But you said I was so much better!"

"You are. But you need time to get used to what happened to you. Why can't you wait a month to move?"

"We're not rich like you, you know. We can't afford to be paying for two places."

He smiled. I suppose he liked being called rich. "You can afford it for just one month," he said.

"There's another thing. Jane—the one person I know

out there—she's leaving for Paris the week after we get there. She's going to live there for a year. But she's going to give a party before they leave. To launch us, so to speak."

"I see. In that case, I think you should go ahead and move when you planned to."

"You think I will be all right?"

He got up to show me to the door. "Yes, I do."

I believed him—because I wanted to. Suddenly, I liked him. "Thank you very much—for everything," I said.

"Good luck," he said. And I felt that he meant it.

I went to the supermarket on Third Avenue one day. An ordinary enough event for most people. For me, it was almost an ordeal.

For the past two years, I had been shopping there several times a week, but when I arrived that morning I felt even more bewildered than I must have the day I first entered it. It is an enormous store, with a layout impossible to grasp at a glance. I pulled out a shopping basket from the row of empty ones in the front section of the store and stood uncertainly behind my basket, while shoppers rushed by to the right and the left of me.

I looked at my list. I had prepared it by copying off most of the items on an old list that I found in a kitchen cabinet and adding the items David had written on the kitchen blackboard. I could remember some of the dishes I used to cook: pot roast, goulash, spaghetti and meatballs, lamb stew, and so forth, but not how to make them. I could have looked up the recipes, but it seemed like too much trouble: there was so much else to do, so much to relearn. So on my list I had mostly staples, and for meat I planned to have only steaks and chops. The list began with the heading PRODUCE. Under produce, I had listed lettuce, cucumbers, oranges, onions, potatoes.

Fine. But where was the produce department? I didn't want to ask anyone at the check-out counter. I was probably a familiar figure to the clerks. They would think I was crazy if suddenly, after two years, I walked up and said, "Excuse me, but could you please tell me where the produce department is?" I could ask another shopper—but could I be sure it wasn't a mother I knew from the playground or a neighbor I was on nodding terms with? I decided to wander around until I found it. I started down the first aisle on the left, and midway down the aisle I saw that a right turn would take me into the produce department. A vestigial memory must have started me off in the correct direction.

I maneuvered my basket over to a bin of oranges and picked out eight. Why eight? I didn't know. Why not eight? I couldn't seem to think of any reason for settling on a particular number. In fact, I couldn't remember if anyone in the family liked oranges. Daddy liked them, I knew that. He had an orange for breakfast every morning, and with it two pieces of toast with Crosse and Blackwell orange marmalade. But did little children eat oranges? More specifically, did *my* little children eat oranges? I didn't know. I moved on to the onion bin and tossed a dozen large yellow onions into my basket. What was I going to do with all those onions? Again, I didn't know. I only knew that in my kitchen there was a drawer, now almost empty, that we called the potato and onion drawer.

I started to put some potatoes into my basket, and then I noticed that the other women were putting them into brown paper bags, so I, too, took a brown paper bag from the shelf and filled it with potatoes. (See how compliant I am! No one would ever know that a week ago—or has it been two weeks, three weeks—I was in a mental hospital.) I picked out a head of lettuce and two cucumbers and was starting toward the next department when the clerk called to me: "Hey!"

I turned around.

"You gotta get those things weighed!"

But of course. I tried to cover my embarrassment with an uneasy laugh. "My, I *am* absentminded today!"

He took the potatoes and onions from me without comment. *It takes all kinds,* his expression implied.

It was cold in the store: too much air conditioning. I was wearing a sleeveless linen shift; my arms were covered with goose bumps. Then I remembered that before I had always brought a sweater with me when I shopped. Good! Another scrap of memory recovered. Maybe tomorrow I will remember how to make goulash.

In the coffee department I had to think: What brand of coffee should I buy? There were so many to choose from! Easily a dozen brands. After studying the cans for a while, it seemed to me that Martinson's had an aura of familiarity. I picked up a can and put it in my basket, not at all sure that David wouldn't say, "Why in the world did you buy Martinson's coffee? You know we always use Savarin."

In the dairy department my impulse was to buy skim milk. But why? Surely my babies were not supposed to drink skim milk? I puzzled over this impulse until at last I remembered: Oh, yes, it is when I am *pregnant* that I drink skim milk. But I am not pregnant now. A woman shopper waiting behind me as I dawdled before the milk compartment could not contain her impatience: "Excuse me, please. *Some* people don't have all day to shop!"

I grabbed four quarts of milk and fled from there, while in my mind I snarled back: *Some* people don't have any manners either!

I wondered, however, if my own manner were noticeably erratic. Wasn't it permissible to hesitate before making a selection? I chose the remaining items on the list as briskly as possible, but at the check-out counter I made another blunder. I told the girl I wanted the groceries delivered and then started to walk out without giving her the address. Of course, anyone might have done that. But it did take the edge off my sense of accomplishment.

Nevertheless, I heard myself reporting proudly to David that evening, "I went to the store today and bought a lot of groceries."

"Good girl!" he said, exactly as he says it to Beth when she has eaten all of her pureed spinach.

My first phone call from Shirley Jaffee since coming home. Or was it the first? I don't know. Perhaps there had been others that I had forgotten. In any case, she called two days—three days?—later to ask us to go to Central Park in the evening, with the Gilberts, for a watermelon picnic.

Shirley and I had a relationship that had developed out of proximity, not much more. She and her husband lived in the same building we did, in an apartment identical to ours but on a higher floor. Unlike most New Yorkers who shy away from neighbors, Shirley had quickly become acquainted with almost everyone in the building by the simple technique of *talking* to people in the elevator and the lobby, instead of merely nodding. She approached me first by asking if I knew of a good cleaner in the neighborhood. She smiled and added ingenuously, "I have only one good dress and I don't want to ruin it." I later learned that her closets were crammed with clothes, her cabinets crowded with heavy silver, fine china and linens; they were hardly the struggling young couple she chose to pretend they were, although Sidney Jaffee was at that time just beginning his psychiatric practice.

Actually, I suppose it was the fact that Sidney was a psychiatrist that caused me to become friendly with the Jaffees. I had never known a psychiatrist socially. I was curious to see if he would act any more sensibly than the rest of us. But he was so young! His boyish face made him look even younger than he was, and his manner was that of a sweet but rather spoiled child. Shirley mothered him and flattered him and spent his earnings at a compulsive pace.

We didn't really see much of the Jaffees until they too had a child. Before that, Shirley was usually out shopping during the day. But after she too had a child to care for—and she did so with devotion—we frequently met in Central Park, with our carriages, and visited each other in the evening. Often David would go with me to their apartment—we'd take turns checking on the children every fifteen minutes. The Jaffees did the same when he accompanied Shirley on her visits to us. David told me that we had spent an evening with the Jaffees two days before I went to the hospital. I was puzzled by the fact that Sidney had not realized that I was in a manic state and called Dr. Stern or told David to. It is one thing for a husband not to realize that his wife has gone crazy, but surely a psychiatrist, one who was well acquainted with my "normal" behavior, should have realized it and done something about it. It is frightening to realize that my children might have seriously injured themselves during those four wild days: I was incapable of being a responsible mother then. In any case, Shirley at least was deeply concerned, David said, when she found out I was in the hospital and had visited me, bringing a jar of sour balls as symbolic chicken soup. I didn't remember her visit—and still don't—nor did I remember the Gilberts.

"Who are the Gilberts?" I asked Shirley. At least I was not embarrassed to display my dulled mind to her. As the wife of a psychiatrist, she must have understood that it was the treatment rather than the illness that had affected my memory.

"You know them. They live below me. They have three children."

"No. I can't remember them."

"They're decorators—they have a shop."

"No, I'm sorry, I don't remember them."

"Well, come with us. You'll remember them when you see them."

She was correct: I did recall them the moment I saw them. With our paraphernalia: a carriage for Deborah Jaffee, a stroller for Beth, a plastic fire engine for Larry, a tricycle for the Gilbert children, and watermelon and paper plates and paper napkins, we straggled over to the park. The children darted in and out among the adults. Their chatter protected me from having to puzzle my way through a conversation with the Gilberts. I remembered them, true, but it was only their looks that were familiar to me.

I knew I had seen this small dark woman leaning against the brick front of our building, watching her children ride their tricycles up and down the block. I remembered the patient boredom of her expression. She never looked cross or tired. On the other hand, she never looked particularly absorbed by their activities. She was merely there, minding them. I remembered envying her: how could she look so crisp, so unstained and unspotted every afternoon? I remembered how clean and cheerful her children always were. "Hello," they always called out to me, adding some news of great importance to them: "We're having ice cream for supper! We bought it at the store!" I could not remember, however, if I used to talk with Mrs. Gilbert or whether my acquaintanceship with her tall, blond husband was more than merely a nodding one.

In the park we sprawled on the grass and messily ate the watermelon. We wiped the children's chins and sticky fingers, and urged them to run off and play so that we could talk—about what?

Sometimes when I wake up in the morning I know I have had a dream, but it eludes me. I move about the kitchen, measuring out coffee into the pot, frowning, thinking. Something about a job I had, was that it? Then a child cries, and the dream scene, which I had almost got hold of, fades away again, irretrievably. In much the same way I could not remember our watermelon party in the park a day or two afterward until David recalled it for me. A fragment remained with me: a free-floating image. I kept thinking of watermelon. I pictured a big melon, ripe almost to bursting. A man's hand plunging a long knife into it. A wedge of melon on a paper plate. Shiny black seeds embedded in the rosy flesh, which faded to white near the rind.

"It's funny," I said to David, "I keep thinking about watermelon. I haven't had any in ages." I was washing glasses, holding each one up to the light for inspection after I rinsed it. David was hanging around the kitchen, not helping, just getting underfoot. I wished he would go away, but since he would stay, I might as well talk to him, I decided.

"Isn't there any beer?" he said as he peered into the refrigerator. He never can find anything in the refrigerator. I don't know why he bothers to look. It would be more honest for him to say, "Please open the refrigerator and get me out a can of beer, because that is what a wife is supposed to do for a husband."

I went over to the refrigerator and immediately found a can of Schlitz. "Here," I said, handing it to him.

He opened it and hoisted himself up onto the butcher's block, his favorite corner of the kitchen.

I plunged my hands into the hot water again and groped for a glass. I could feel David's eyes on me as he spoke. "You had watermelon Sunday afternoon. In the park. Don't you remember?"

I looked down at the glass I held. A martini glass with a shallow bowl, a fragile stem, the only survivor now from a set of eight. "Well, I do keep thinking about watermelon, but I can't remember having any."

"We went with the Jaffees and the Gilberts. We took the kids."

He had opened the viewfinder for me. Now I saw the watermelon on the grass, a clump of children circling it, Bob Gilbert cutting into the melon with the long, sharp knife of my image. Still, it was a partial memory, a scene from a silent movie, a glimpse into a kaleidoscope.

"I guess I remember. It's all blurred though."

He drank his beer in silence. If he is human, he must have been thinking: How long is she going to be like this? I wanted to say: David, David, help me, tell me I'll be all right soon, tell me I'll stop forgetting things. But I didn't. He had worked all day. He was tired. He needed peace. A wife in one piece. *I must stop leaning on him.* I tried to force myself to think of nothing but the stains on the glasses I was washing. My stains: lipstick stains. Lipstick is stubborn; it is hard to wash off. David drinks more than I do, but he doesn't stain the glasses; he breaks them. Men are like that. They can't help it, I guess; they just break things.

I don't break glasses, but I broke down. They have raped my mind, those men in the hospital. I will never be the same, never be intact again. They said everything would come back to me—but it hasn't. And I am still forgetting. They didn't tell me it would be like that. *What else didn't they tell me?*

"Are you crying?"

"No," I said, as I wiped away my tears with a corner of the dishtowel.

He jumped down from the butcher's block, landed on the floor with a thump. All solid and sane, he opened his arms to me. "You are crying. There's nothing to cry about now. It's over."

"But it isn't. I still keep forgetting."

"Talk to Dr. Rosen about it tomorrow. You'll see, it will be all right. I promise you."

"Who are you, God or something?"

"Ah, darling, I only wish I could be."

When the telephone rang, I was sitting on my bed cutting my toenails with a pair of manicure scissors. My nails were long and ragged, neglected, like so many other things in my life, during my stay in the hospital.

"Hello?" a faint, unfamiliar, feminine voice asked.

"Hello," I said.

"This is Johnny Fishman's wife, Paula."

"Oh, hello!" In the instant it took to utter that, in a voice that rang false even to me, my thoughts ran wildly ahead: Johnny Fishman, Johnny Fishman, who is he? Aha, I've got it, now I remember. He wears dark glasses even at night. But is he married? Did I know that? Do I know his wife? Is this her way of telling me they just got married?

Her voice, still faint, was shy and formal: "We're having a party on the thirtieth and we'd like for you and Dave to come."

"Oh, we can't," I blurted out. "We're moving. To New Jersey." (How much did she know of me? Did I know her at all? Maybe I had seen her and told her all about our house.)

"Oh, I'm so sorry you're moving," my unknown, perhaps friend said. "Everyone's leaving New York! It's terrible. You know that we've moved?"

It was like playing blindman's buff, trying to talk to this girl I may or may not have known. "Listen," I said. "The baby's screaming. I have to run. Sorry about the party."

"Oh, I am too—but let's get together before you leave."

"Sure," I said, knowing that I was lying. "Thanks for calling."

In the evening, again the reconstruction. I, as usual, stretched out on the couch, David, as usual, in the big orange chair, smoking his pipe, drinking bourbon.

"Dave?"

"Ummmm."

"Did you know Johnny Fishman was married?"

"Yes, dear."

"Who did he marry?"

"You know her. We went to a party for them."

I cast out my torn fishnet of a mind and came up— with nothing.

"She called me today. They're having a party. She said, 'I'm Johnny Fishman's wife.' I didn't know whether to say, oh, since when and good luck or how are you or what. It's so awful, trying to talk to someone when you can't even remember whether you know her or not."

"Lots of people forget things. You only met her once. At Ilya's. Don't you remember we brought a salami—as a wedding present? Everyone brought crazy things like that."

A small, dark, crowded room. Lots of smoke. Too
many people. Christmas carols and glasses of punch, too
sweet, too strong, everyone swirling around, a short girl
with the legs of a dancer and short dark hair cut in bangs
and big breasts protruding from a low-cut black dress.
All the men trying not to stare at her breasts. All the
men and the women too wondering how did homely
Johnny get a girl like that? All in a rush I remembered:
Ilya, Johnny, Paula, Cliff, Eve, Tony, Irene, Mario, so
many people, so many faces I had forgotten.

"Yes, yes, I do remember! We all drank too much
punch. It was sickening!"

Again, David's reassuring: "You see, I told you it will
all come back."

Again, my cry of despair: "Oh, but you don't know
what it's like—it's like waking up—*but all day long!*"

One morning I was looking through my wallet for the
picture of the house we were buying. I thought that if I
studied it long enough, I might begin to remember
something about it. I did not find the picture—it was in
my wallet, I know, but I stopped looking for it when I
came across something else that interested me more.
Three pieces of paper, each covered with my handwriting: notes that I had made while in the hospital. The
first page read as follows:

In admitting room dr handed D the bill—"I feel eu-
phoric with intermittent waves of anxiety" Exhausted,
forced into routine—visiting hours in the day room—

Elsie Dinsmore on the piano stool—from time to time
removed for physical exam—Norwegian physical exam
—Day room the girl who keeps saying "shock treat-
ment," "my psychiatrist" blurrr—waking up 3 doctors
who told me "Trust me" you will not have shock treat-
ment unless permission House Dr, my dr, dr who did
physical all said I wouldn't have—but I did—why lie
—why not say you will have an injection and not re-
member anything—now I have no trust in anything—
stribbed of all powers of decision making except which
of 3 dresses to wear, who would not falter
The underground—

All of the above was written on the inside of an envelope that had been torn open. I had no recollection
of writing it, but I was pleased to see that except for the
misspelling of "stripped" and the ominous sound of
the last two words it sounded rational enough. Indeed, I
rather liked the way I had apparently described my
condition to the examining doctor: "I feel euphoric with
intermittent waves of anxiety." I did not understand the
reference to Elsie Dinsmore. That is to say, I remembered
the scene in the book but did not know what relationship it had to me. I suppose I had been forced to remain
in the dayroom, just as Elsie was forced to remain on the
piano stool. But she was kept there by her father whom
she had disobeyed rather than violate the Sabbath by
playing the piano as he had demanded. And I was kept
in the dayroom only because the hospital routine re-

quired it, not because I had done anything wrong. The
reference, I thought, is not apt.

"The underground"—why did I break off there? What
dark thought was to follow?

The other two pages of notes were on typing paper.
Evidently they were written somewhat later. I have
copied them down exactly as I found them:

> *The RT aide—6 ft, buxom, jovial—getting a degree
> at City College Angela—oh, please, won't you take
> me home—somebody please, take me home— Did you
> buy that dress here or on the outside? Nurse, I want to
> see my doctor—is that shrill agitated voice mine? I
> must act my best, so that I can move to three*
> *6—12—*
> *no water, no food, talk, cigarette, money, sex, mind,
> beauty, all basics—poor, rich, the Greek girl loves Jews,
> the Italian girl has an Italian doctor Afterwards—no
> recollection of anything—where I am, date, the city, all
> names a blur. "You had a nervous breakdown," some-
> one tells me— "Nonsense! Impossible!" I say— From
> what? Gradually reality seeps back The plant in the
> corner— It is mine I remember my husband brought
> it to me. Later in RT we play bingo and I win some
> writing paper. I write a note to David—but what else
> did I say—I don't even remember— Carol and I play
> dominoes—a dull game—then scrabble—more interest-
> ing—I would like to talk to the surly young man but
> he avoids me— Morning I wait for treatment, but end-
> lessly. Awakened at 6 for temperature—wash, don't get
> dressed. I write a letter to Dr. Stern and then complain
> —why am I not on the third floor—why not given a*

pass why not all kinds of things I'm sick of hearing women curse and shriek—sick of smoking on an empty stomach—can't wait to see Dr. Rosen but I want to see Dr. Stern, David, my children more, my darling babies, I keep looking at their pictures—I wonder what David is telling everybody— Remember to tell Dr. Rosen to speak to David about not making me put everything back.

Pacing up and down—Aline: you see, I was raped—I don't want to have shock treatment because I might forget what he looks like—he put on my card delusions of pregnancy—but I really am pregnant—you see I have this huge vagina You had the shock treatment yet —the word itself onamatopoeia—vibrates thru the room weirdly

The aide—how much you pay for that dress? "Fourteen dollars" "Fourteen dollars! Where at?" "Altman's." "Man, that's too much, one little ole dress!" "You stop kissing your husband, you make me jealous!" "Come on, you kiss him, too! I'm generous— You can share him!" "Yarss"—the doctor who went to Harvard. Brown and white checked suit. All right ladies RT! (In RT we dance the cha cha! Try to work a crossword puzzle. Sing songs. "What are you in for?" a surly handsome young man asks me.

At first, it was like reading someone else's diary, reading those notes. I read them a second time, and then a third. It seemed to me then that I could remember Aline. Short, slightly built, with long, black hair and a ghostly complexion. Or was that Angela? The Norwegian doctor was very blond and young. An intern, perhaps.

The R.T. aide was a Negro, with a laugh as rich as Karo.

The effort to force the return of my memory left me feeling tired and somewhat depressed. I folded up the notes and put them away in my desk drawer. Then I went out to buy some groceries. I could not stop thinking of that strange phrase "the underground." What had I to do with subterranean tunnels? My life has always been open and aboveboard. It is not conducted by secret or stealthy means. At the store I bought a steak for dinner and a loaf of bread. When I got home, the children were having lunch. I went into the kitchen to help Victoria and had to stop burrowing into the tunnels of my mind. Remember what Dr. Rosen said: It's not important that I recover every memory. Remember what David says: It's over now. Everything will be all right.

Why me? Everyone thinks that when any disaster strikes. But, really, why me?

The apartment was quiet. Victoria had stuffed Beth's fat, protesting arms and legs and round body into a stretch suit and snapped and buttoned Larry into his clothes and jammed them both into the stroller and off they had gone to the park, trailing a red balloon and a quacking duck. I had an hour and a half to myself.

I should start packing, I thought. There's so much to be done. Every night, when David comes home, he says, "Well, what did you do today?" I can't say I sat on the couch with a cup of coffee and thought: Why me? I am supposed to say, "I cleaned out the hall closet and threw away all the old letters I have been carrying around for years." But he is kind to me because I have had a breakdown, so when I say, "Nothing much," he does not ask for more details.

Why me? I remember once saying to David, "Adrienne's going to crack up. I just know it . . . that wild laugh, almost hysterical. Those overly dramatic gestures. The way she's always flinging her arms about . . ." That was at least four years ago. She doesn't seem to have calmed down any, but while I was having shock treatments, she was driving around in the suburbs, in a station wagon full of groceries and children and wet bathing suits and sandy sneakers. She was meeting her husband at the train and driving him home to a steak dinner on the patio, and tucking the children into bed, saying, "Hush, now, Mommy will be right here, in the living room with Daddy."

And I? What have I been doing? I have done those things I ought not to have done. What things? I don't know. I just know I have done wrong. That is my general confession. Where is my prayer book? Is it at home or here? David doesn't like it when I refer to my former home as "home." But that is how I think of it. My prayer book must still be there. Mother never throws anything out. I haven't looked at it in years. I can't even remember the general confession anymore. I said it hundreds of times, kneeling on a prayer bench, my father beside me. My prayer book has a white leather cover, and I used to clean it with shoe polish. The polish would rub

off on my hands, and while the minister read the ser-
mon, I would scrub my hands with my handkerchief,
like Lady Macbeth, scrubbing away at those damned
spots.

I ought to be cleaning now. The closet. Or the crisper
drawer. If I open the crisper drawer, I know what I'll
find: celery gone limp in the stalk, brown in the leaves.
A forgotten scrap of onion. Some pears that have never
ripened and never will. Three lemons that looked fresh
at first glance, but one at least will have rotted on its un-
derside.

David is always saying to me, "Why don't you clean
out the refrigerator?" Another wife might say, "It's none
of your business why I don't clean the refrigerator." But
I go and clean it out. My sister Martha reacts the same
way. We obey when our husbands scold. Or cry. We are
weak. Why? Why did I have to have a breakdown?

My coffee was cold. There was still time to start on the
closet before the children came home. Instead I went
over to the bookcase and took down an encyclopedia. I
put it on the dining room table and looked through it
until I found the listing for shock treatment. I skimmed
through the article. I was not much interested in who
had discovered the treatment or under what circum-
stances. I read that electric shock has had great success in
treating involutional melancholia, and that shock treatment is often used to make the psychotic patient rational
enough for psychotherapy.

The psychotic patient. I read through the entry again,

this time carefully. I could find no reference to the *neurotic* patient. But I am not psychotic. I had a nervous breakdown. At least, that is what they told me . . . in the hospital, the nurses, the doctors, and David, he, too, said it was just a nervous breakdown, a minor one. I turned back to the book and read the dreadful line again: *Shock treatment is often used to make the psychotic patient rational enough for psychotherapy.* I closed the book and put it away, but where could I put the new fear that I had found in it? Am I psychotic? Perhaps they all lied to me. All those doctors, David, the well-tailored, well-heeled Dr. Rosen. He said for me to call him whenever I needed to. I will call him and ask him: "Am I psychotic?" But if I am, is he likely to say, "Why, yes, as a matter of fact, you're off your rocker. We've arrested the disease, but it's just a question of time before you're back in the hospital again."

My little boy says to me when we are walking on the street, "What's that?" and I say, "That's a truck," and he says, "That's a truck," and then he points to the same truck and says, "What's that?" because he wants to hear me say again, "That's a truck." I got up and went to the telephone because I was like my little boy: I wanted to ask a question, even though I already knew the answer it would receive.

Surprisingly, I got through to him right away; he was not at the hospital, or at his other office in the suburbs, or too busy with a patient to speak to me.

He sounded pleased to hear from me. "How are you, dear?"

"All right. Look, this is what I want to know. Am I psychotic?"

"Absolutely not! What makes you ask?"

"I looked up shock treatment in an encyclopedia. It said it was used with psychotics. It didn't say anything about using it with neurotics."

"How old is the encyclopedia?"

"A few years—I don't know exactly—but look, if I am psychotic, you wouldn't tell me anyway, would you?"

"What makes you think that?"

"Well, it just doesn't sound like something you would tell a patient."

"Why not?"

"It's so awful to be psychotic—if someone didn't know he was, wouldn't it be cruel to tell him?"

"Do you know the definition of a psychosis?"

I thought for a moment. I tried to remember the definitions I had memorized for my mental hygiene course in college many years ago. "It's much more serious than a neurosis—and aren't psychoses incurable?"

"No, you're absolutely wrong about that. A great many psychoses can be permanently cured." He made a little speech about the recent dramatic advances in the treatment of psychoses, studded with percentages and references to various clinics and hospitals and drugs. I listened with a growing sense of doom and interrupted him when I could stand it no longer: "Why are you bothering to tell me all about psychoses if I'm not psychotic?"

He laughed. "You're a sharp one, aren't you? Why don't you believe me when I tell you that you're not?"

I remembered the scraps of paper I had found in my wallet. "Why should I believe you? You've lied to me before. I found some notes I made in the hospital. They said that three doctors had told me I was not going to have shock treatment and then I had it. As I said in the notes, why lie, why not tell a person what's going to happen? Because when you find out someone has lied to you once, then you don't have any faith in him ever."

He said, "We didn't lie to you, dear. At the time when you were first admitted, we thought we would be able to treat you with drugs. But after the first day I could see you weren't responding to them satisfactorily. So we had to go to shock treatment."

Good-bye, dear darling Dr. Rosen. I thanked him, put down the telephone, and humming, went back to the living room. What was I humming? I smiled when I identified it: it was a line from Handel's *Messiah*: "I know that my redeemer liveth."

I started trying to read the newspaper daily, in an effort toward resuming my place in the world. Even if I didn't get out to the current plays and movies and concerts and art shows, I could at least familiarize myself with a few *au courant* names so that I wouldn't have to keep saying, "Who's he?" in conversations with friends who visited us.

I did not find it easy to read, however. When I tried to skim through a news article, an inner voice had to sound each word. This slowed me down, and frequently, if the article was trivial, it did not seem worth the effort. I thought perhaps I should sign up for one of those courses advertised on buses and subways: NOW, READ A NOVEL IN AN HOUR! I wondered what novel they meant. *War and Peace? À la Recherche du Temps Perdu?*

In the hospital people brought me books, but I couldn't concentrate enough to read them. At home I was able to settle my attention on the words in the paper, but so often they were meaningless. There was no point to trying to read the paper unless David was around to fish me out of the muddles I fell into while reading. Example: I plodded through an article on Lyndon B. Johnson. It was the writer's opinion that he was sure to receive the Democratic Party's nomination at the coming convention. When I had finished reading the article, I said to David in the untroubled voice I use to ask any reasonable question: "I don't understand. Doesn't Kennedy want to be reelected?"

David was very good at handling such moments. He made his voice as matter-of-fact as his explanations: "Kennedy is dead. He was shot last November—in Dallas."

But of course. Everyone knows that. Another large fact

I had forgotten. My reaction was always the same: a kind of slow, agonized mental blush. I could never believe that David was not as frightened as I was by the incidents. It was all very well to keep saying, "Your memory will come back"—but would it? I wondered.

David was puzzled because I was not more reticent about my breakdown. He was home one morning when Mildred called to ask me to meet her in the park. Her little girl, Dee-Dee, was Larry's favorite playmate, and the four of us, and later, after Beth was born, the five of us, had spent many mornings together in Central Park.

I didn't know Mildred very well. We had met in the park, drawn into conversation by boredom and the interest our children displayed in each other. What I knew of her, however, I liked. She appeared to be about my age, which appealed to me because I was a little self-conscious about being a rather elderly young mother, especially in the face of all those *Redbook* magazine ads that kept telling me I was old. And she, too, was a writer. She had worked for a television network for many years, but I felt that she had taken to her new role of housewife and mother with more ease and grace than I had. I loved my children, but this did nothing to alter the fact that I found it extremely boring to sit on a bench in Central Park for four or five hours a day.

Mildred said that she was bored too, but she looked happy. She was a short, graying brunette, with a plain, friendly face, a dowdy way of dressing. I was often tempted

babies, etc.) The second paragraph: more sweet noth-ings. We think of you all the time and long to see the darling children . . .

The third paragraph: "Darling, we simply cannot un-derstand how you can let more than a month go by with-out writing your parents, when you know your poor father cannot get out and of course I don't go off and leave him, and every day we hope and pray to hear from you, but now it has been over a month and we have not heard from you."

I put the letter down. One page fell to the floor, but I did not bother to pick it up. How could I possibly an-swer that accusation? Could I write: Dear Mother and Daddy, I am sorry that I have not written, but I had a nervous breakdown four days after I got back, and I had to have shock treatment and stay in the hospital for a month, and in fact, I forgot all about you until just a few days ago when I got home, and even then I never thought you might be waiting to hear from me. I have been busy trying to remember how to make the chil-dren's breakfast and how to get to Bloomingdale's and who is President of the United States.

Of course I could never tell them. I hadn't even thought before that moment: Do they know? Thank God I had not called *them* at five in the morning. For the first time I began to wonder how I had acted at home. Was I already manic while I was there? David had not been with me. I couldn't ask my parents. One more puzzle to be solved.

I'll write them soon, maybe tomorrow, I promised my conscience, which was now fully awake. As soon as I can think of an explanation for my silence. All day, as I sorted the dirty clothes and stuffed socks into the washer and emptied the ashes from David's pipe into the overflowing garbage bag in the kitchen, I carried with me, like a whining child clinging to my leg, my mother's querulous voice, marveling that any child could be so inconsiderate as to not write for more than a month, for land's sake, anybody could find time for a line or two, and my father's voice, more hurt than angry, saying— now it was I who was deaf, not he. Strain though I might, I could not hear what he said.

A few days later, I went with David to the "closing" for our new house. I didn't want to go because I could not remember the house at all and I did not look forward to having to bluff my way through the meeting. But my signature was needed, so I had to go.

"Do they know about me?" I asked David as we rode in a taxi to the train station.

"Abrahms doesn't. But I'm not sure about MacDonald. He was very upset when we had to postpone the closing. I told him you were confined to the hospital— back trouble, I said—but I was so upset then myself— I'm not sure I didn't say something to make him suspicious."

I wondered whether MacDonald would stare at me, looking for telltale signs to confirm his suspicions. If he did, I was not aware of it. I moved like a sleepwalker through the proceedings. First to see Abrahms, who is our lawyer, in his office. That part was easy. There, I had only to greet him, say I had been fine, thank you, ask after his family, not remembering, until David told me later, that I have known his wife and children for years, and then sign a few papers.

I have often been told that one should read whatever one signs, but it did not bother me at all to sign those documents without even glancing at them. Just as in the hospital, I did as I was told, I felt no need to take responsible action.

I sat at a table in Abrahms' office, humming softly, waiting to be told what to do next. David watched me, the way a parent watches a small child on a social occasion, hoping that he will make a good impression.

"I'm thirsty," I said once, and instantly he was out of his chair and on his way to the water cooler to fetch me a paper cup of water. Was he afraid that I might throw a tantrum if he did not move quickly?

Abrahms did not approve of our buying the house. He thought we were paying too much for it. Interspersed into his remarks concerning the various papers were phrases meant to let us know what he really thought: "Well, if you still want to go through with this deal . . ." "If you really want to close . . ."

I had no opinion. How can you know whether or not you really want to buy a house if you do not remember ever seeing it? Actually, the question was merely rhetorical. We had either to go ahead and buy the house or forfeit our large deposit.

So we signed the papers and drove with Abrahms to MacDonald's law office to sign some more papers there.

MacDonald, who wore a blue shirt with a button-down collar and a seersucker suit, was more sociable than Abrahms, who remained as gloomily businesslike as his dark suit and vest. MacDonald slipped his arm around me while greeting me, said I was looking wonderful without really looking at me, and removed his arm from around my waist at exactly the moment when I began to grow uncomfortable under its pressure.

I said, "Oh, thank you," in response to his compliment, and I said, "How is your family?" and he said, "Fine, thank you," and then I said, "Is there a ladies' room I could use?" because my palms were damp and I thought that my nose must be shiny, and I wanted to get away before he said, "What kind of back trouble did you have, to have to stay in the hospital so long?"

I had no answer prepared for such a question. If I had known before what David had told him, I would have asked Dr. Stern to tell me something plausible to say about back trouble. I washed my hands and powdered my face and freshened my lipstick and combed my hair in the tiny lavatory down the hall from MacDonald's office, while reading and rereading the crudely hand-lettered sign on the wall over the basin: PLEASE LEAVE THIS REST ROOM AS YOU WOULD LIKE TO FIND IT. Then

there was nothing to do but join the men in MacDonald's office.

They were seated around an old-fashioned oak office
table. MacDonald jumped up when I came in. Abrahms
reluctantly imitated him. David, reading through one
of the papers, remained seated but smiled encouragingly
at me. I sat down in the chair that MacDonald pulled
out for me and signed my name a few more times. In the
intervals between signing, I occupied myself with studying MacDonald. He is only passably good-looking. His
ears protrude a bit too much. His nose looks as though
it must have been broken once (a fall from a horse,
perhaps?). His coloring is nondescript: light brown hair,
hazel eyes. Yet his manner is that of a man who has had
great success with women.

David asked a question about one of the papers, and
I chided myself for having such frivolous thoughts while
he was grappling with the legal details of house buying. He sighed frequently, while I, his wife, his partner
in the venture, sat there feeling as detached as the pretty
young secretary who brought in a final paper for us to
sign.

At last it was done. We had "closed." The house was
ours. David and I sat there and smiled at each other.
Abrahms congratulated us and somewhat doubtfully
wished us luck. MacDonald made jokes about home own-
ing. ("Now your troubles begin! Wait until you wake up
one morning all snowed in! You'll wish you were back
in New York." "How are you at lawn mowing? Got your

muscles in shape?") We said good-bye and thank you very much to Abrahms. Then David, McDonald, and I got into his Volkswagen to ride out to the house, my house, that as far as my memory knew, I had never seen.

MacDonald, who seemed afraid of silence, talked continually as he drove, mostly of the house and matters concerning it. David, for the most part, was silent. I knew that it saddened him that I was incompletely present for what should have been a momentous occasion. He had said several times, using the identical words each time, "I grew up in a three-room apartment. You don't know what this means to me: to own a house, a beautiful house with trees and grounds . . ." His voice trailed off. His wonderment was so large it overwhelmed him. He would have liked for me to share his feelings. Instead he had an automaton for a wife, who had dressed herself attractively for the event, and who had smiled when smiled at, and who had signed her name in a hand that was almost steady, but who had been empty of any feelings, except: Am I acting all right? Does MacDonald know about me?

MacDonald said he had had a cleaning woman in after they moved out. He hoped I would find the place in good shape. In fact, he was sure I would. This woman had cleaned for his family for years. She used to work for his aunt full-time. Now she did only day work now and then. She had arthritis, so she only worked when she felt well enough. She didn't need to work: she had a nice little house in the colored section. Her son worked for a friend of MacDonald's who is a builder. Her daughter was a cook for one of the wealthiest families in town.

"Ummmm," I murmured.

MacDonald knows everyone in town. He can never mention anyone without giving a brief biographical sketch of him. I wondered, as he drove along the narrow, curving country roads with skillful carelessness, what he was saying around town about me. Evidently he thought himself exempt from speed limits; probably he had a similar disrespect for a person's privacy.

I had no idea how far from town the house was and did not know when we turned into our road that it *was* our road. David said heartily, for my benefit, "Well, here's our road. Hon, did you ever think you'd be living on Appletree Road?"

As we turned in, I saw first the cows, dappled cows sitting peacefully, ponderously in the pastureland of a large farm.

"Glory be to God for dappled things," I said to David. A quotation I overuse: Hopkins is one of my favorite poets.

"What did you say?" MacDonald asked, turning toward me for a dangerous moment while the car swerved round a curve.

"I said Larry will like the cows."

"Yes, Peggy loved them."

Cornfields, pastureland, red barns and silos, apple orchards, land that dipped and rose again, in the distance, soft blue hills. Sunshine and clean blue sky. The kind of scene you find more often in children's picture books than in life itself, now that turnpikes, throughways, split-level developments, and Howard Johnsons have taken over.

David looked at me expectantly.

"It's lovely," I said. "Even more lovely than I remembered." I thought: I never used to be able to lie well. Lately, it seems as natural as the truth.

"You know that spot on the bedroom ceiling?" MacDonald said, as we continued to bounce along the road.

"Ummm."

"I've had it plastered over. You'd never know it was there. Do you like the color of those walls, by the way?"

"Oh, yes," I said, rather too enthusiastically. After all, perhaps they were purple or chartreuse. Politeness could be overdone.

"I had that color specially mixed. How will it go with your things? It would be a shame to paint over it."

David saved me. "I think it's a lovely shade of blue."

Dear David, thank you, David. "Unfortunately," I said smoothly, "our bedroom in the city is green and gold, so we'll have some redecorating to do."

We turned into a gravel driveway lined with elms. MacDonald braked abruptly. To the left of the driveway was—the house pictured in the photograph I had been carrying in my wallet, "our" house. I tried out the phrase in my mind. My first thought was: Oh, the shutters are black. I had assumed they were green. My surprise was so great that for an instant I thought I had spoken aloud. Nobody moved for a moment. Nobody said anything. The wind rustled the leaves of "our" trees. Silence, except for the wind in the trees, the faint growl of a tractor off in the distance. I wondered what David was thinking. Was his heart pounding like mine? MacDonald, usually a fast-moving man, seemed caught up in the moment with us. But after all, it had been his house. It had been home to his child since birth. Now it was ours.

He was the first to move. He climbed out of the car and came around to open the other door for me. "Well, here you are. Home, sweet home!"

We all stood around uncertainly on the lawn for a few minutes. MacDonald rocked up and down on his heels and jiggled the change in his pocket. David kept looking at me, rather than the house, and once he put his hand out toward me, as though to steady me. I wished I could go into the house alone. I did not want to walk in for the "first" time with MacDonald at my elbow.

He was not a man to remain idle for long. "Well, shall we go in?" he said. We followed him across the lawn and into the house.

A large square room with white plaster walls and mellowed pine floors that squeaked as you walked on them. Long windows that let in lozenges of afternoon sun. A large brick fireplace. Beyond this room another, almost its twin, with an identical fireplace, a bay of windows overlooking the backyard and the meadow beyond, "our" meadow. Then, into the hallway, past the staircase, to the kitchen, large as our living room in the city. Our footsteps were loud in the empty rooms. If only MacDonald would stop talking about plasterers and beams and roofing and insulation, and just let me look in peace. I opened and closed two kitchen cabinets, just to have something to do with my hands. The cabinets were bare except for clean white paper lining the shelves. MacDonald's wife was evidently an excellent housekeeper.

We wandered out to the hall again. "It's a beautiful house," I said to David. He was hovering near me, as though I were a toddler who might slip on the freshly waxed floors.

He smiled gratefully at me.

"After you," MacDonald said, when we paused in front of the stairs. All three of us climbed the stairs and gravely inspected the four large corner bedrooms. "Ours," the front one above the living room, had a fireplace, and so did the one above the dining room.

"Larry's room," David said quickly when I entered it and exclaimed involuntarily, "Oh, another fireplace." He had drawn a plan of the house several times and told me who was to have what room. But he correctly surmised that I had forgotten most of what he had told me.

I don't remember much more about that first trip to the house. I suppose we didn't stay there very long.

How much time can you spend just walking around in empty rooms?

MacDonald drove us back into town. David told me later that he bought us a drink in a bar, a German rathskeller kind of place, but I don't remember that. I don't know why some parts of that day are as sharply present as this very moment, and why other parts have faded away as thoroughly as a forgotten dream.

I do remember that we spoke very little on the train going back to the city. Two or three times David said, "You really like it then?"

We were sitting in a crowded car, where smoking was permitted. My eyes smarted. I hoped he wouldn't think I was fighting back tears. "Oh, yes," I said, each time he asked.

I did like the house and the trees and the barn and the acres and acres of meadowland. But my feelings were free-floating—not anchored to anything in my past. Event had followed event in the usual order. First we looked at the house, then we talked about it for a day or so and decided to make an offer, then MacDonald refused the offer, then more talking, a second call from us, this time offering to buy at the price he asked, then a trip to MacDonald's office to leave a deposit, then anxious weeks of financing, weighing one mortgage offer against another, then, finally, the closing. I knew that all of this had happened because David had told me so. But shock treatment had robbed me of all but the culmination, the closing. It was like climbing a flight of stairs to the landing, and then finding, when you looked back over your shoulder, that the stairs you had climbed had vanished. I leaned my head back against the dirty red plush of the seat and closed my eyes and lost myself in the rhythm of the train until we reached the city.

Soon after the closing, I began the preparations for moving. I started by going through the laundry hampers in search of odds and ends of clothes that should be thrown out, not just left to lie until some vague future time when I might feel desperate enough to wear them. I pulled out a chartreuse and white cotton knit shirt that I had never liked. It had an odd, fussy neckline, a deep curve outlined with small white buttons, and was in excellent condition despite the fact that it had been jammed into the hamper for three years or more.

Throw it away! In my mind, I could hear David saying this. He is quite ruthless about getting rid of nonessentials. He plunges vigorously into the debris of my life and pitches out the useless with the same ease with which he hacks off friendships that have withered and tosses out a galosh that has lost its mate. In his studio his equipment is arranged with compulsive neatness. When he no longer likes a photograph, he destroys it, and the negative too, and that's that.

One day, for instance, he found me squatting on my heels before my bedroom closet. I held a pair of brown alligator shoes, hopelessly out of style, in my hands.

"Should I throw these out or shouldn't I? I can't decide."

He bent down and took the shoes from me. "Here. I'll decide for you."

I followed the sound of his footsteps to the back door, listened as he opened the door, heard my shoes land in the garbage can, winced as he slammed the back door (why can't he ever just close it?), waited for his return, for I knew that he would come back to me, back to the bedroom where I still squatted before the squalor of my closet, poking around in it like an old gypsy woman raking among coals for portents of good or evil.

"There! You'll never miss them. But *you* would have gone on keeping them forever."

He is right, I thought.

I am starting a new life now.

I am moving to the country.

They have cut away great chunks of my old life.

My mind is clean and tidy now.

All right. I will start over again. In the country, where everything will be clean and tidy and almost empty, not dense and dirty, as it is in the city.

I will throw away this green and white shirt.

I will model myself after David.

He will be my apostle.

But he and all those other clear-cut people will never know the higgledy-piggledy pleasure of poking around among your own remains and finding—but what is this?

I pulled out a black sweater. I am not overly fastidious, but this sweater was more than soiled—it was filthy. It smelled of tobacco smoke and sweat. Whoever had been wearing it had spilled food on it and allowed it to dry into crusts. Hair and lint clogged its loose weave. One large silver button hung from a single strand of thread; another was missing. Where had this sweater come from? Surely it hadn't been left at our place by a friend. I don't know anyone who wears such dirty clothes. A cleaning woman perhaps? I couldn't remember who had cleaned for me before I went to the hospital. I held it up to me to judge the size. It was a big sweater, too big certainly for Victoria, and anyway, she was always immaculate. More my size.

My size.

Mine?

I slipped it on. It fit perfectly. The stink of the sweater enclosed me. I took it off quickly and stuffed it back into the hamper.

In the evening I took a long bath. I lay back in the warm tub of water and deliberately thought about nothing much for a while. Then I shaved my armpits and my legs, being careful to get all the hairs in the hard-to-get-at places: around the knobs of the knees and in back of them. I dried myself and dusted my body with talcum powder, and then I dried my razor carefully, the way David had taught me, and I put it on the top shelf of the medicine cabinet. (Keep medicines and sharp tools out of the reach of children!) Then, wearing my flowered nylon robe and holding the filthy black sweater, I approached David, who was sitting in the orange chair in the living room, studying some sheets of contact prints.

He didn't look up. He didn't notice that my hair was curly from the steam in the bathroom and that I was wearing my prettiest robe and that I had not yet put any cold cream on—just in case. I was ready for bed—and for him, if he wanted me, but there was one thing I had to get straight first.

"Is this mine?"

"Yes," he said, without even looking up.

"It's filthy."

"It's no wonder. You wore it every day in the hospital. The air conditioning was too cold."

"Why didn't you bring me another one?"

Exasperated at being interrupted, he put the prints down and turned to me. "Look. I had a lot to do. You didn't care that your sweater was dirty. You didn't even take a bath for two weeks. I finally had to say to the nurse, 'Can't you do something to make her take a bath? She takes one every night at home.' So the nurse said okay, and she must have told you to take baths, because after that you did. But, Jesus, you didn't care your sweater was dirty."

"I'm sorry I interrupted you."

Ashamed of his outburst, he smiled at me. "It's all right. I know things are confusing for you. I'll help you as much as I can."

"Do your work."

He had made amends, so he picked up the prints

again. He did not see me leave the room. He did not hear me open the back door and throw away the filthy black sweater. Later, all clean and tidy, I slid between the sheets of my bed and lay there, alone and empty. I had to go to sleep with the new knowledge that once I was so crazy I could not even keep myself clean.

Count sheep. Don't think.

One, two, three, four, five, six sheep jump over a fence.

I wonder who invented that device.

It doesn't work.

Baa, baa, black sheep, have you any wool?

Yes, sir, yes, sir, three bags full.

Black wool for a filthy black sweater.

I threw it away. Don't think about it. Start over. A clean new country life. Cattle grazing in fields. The fresh smell of cut grass. They raise sheep around there, too, David says.

One, two, three, four, five, six, seven, eight, nine, ten, eleven, twelve . . . I felt drowsy. Thank God for Elavil . . .

My first visit to Dr. Stern "after the fall." I hadn't seen Arthur Miller's play, but in the cab, on the way there, I thought of the impending visit in that way: the first time after the fall. Miller's play is reputed to be about Marilyn Monroe, who committed suicide. Suicide has sometimes attracted me: a sign of weakness. Why struggle? Just give in, go to sleep. What restrains me is my feeling that no one else could ever love my children as much as I do. For a long time Dr. Stern would not prescribe sleeping pills for me. When I pointed out that I could obtain a prescription from any general practitioner, he relented. Once he mailed me a prescription for some drug—I've forgotten its name—with the wry notation: "You are now in Marilyn Monroe's class." Although I was pleased that he had included a note with the prescription, I didn't like the comparison. She killed herself. Did he think that someday I would also?

At his building, the same white-haired doorman as always was leaning against a wall in the outer foyer. Did he wonder at seeing me year after year? He always greeted me with the friendly deference reserved for those known to the building. Once I tipped him for getting me a cab and he grew embarrassed, protesting, "Oh, no, miss."

Miss, not madam. At least to the white-haired I was still young enough to be called miss.

I walked past him, through the main lobby: clean, old-fashioned West Side lobby, not quite luxurious. "Antique" mirrors. Marble floor. Clack-clack of my heels on the marble floor. Dim light, ought to take off my sunglasses, but that means fumbling in my bag for the case. I rang the bell (chimes, not a bell, more "refined"). RING BELL, WALK IN, the sign said. I did so.

Red walls rushed toward me. I stepped into the room and was enclosed by them. Not a room, but a womb: those red walls formed a placenta, protecting, nourishing me. Across the room, a lamp illuminated a tank of tropical fish. The windows were closed; draperies, tightly woven, but tissue thin, concealed the view. I sat down, but felt as though I floated in fluid.

No one else was there. Good. I did not have to duck my head, look the other way in order not to stare. I did not have to pretend to be absorbed in a magazine I had already read.

I was barely seated when the door to the inner office opened. Early. At least ten minutes before appointment time. Good! He couldn't wait to see me. Couldn't sit there alone writing bills or making notes about the condition of the last patient or scanning medical journals or working on a chess problem. He had to come out. Good!

"Hello!" His greeting was expansive, like that of a host rather than a doctor.

"Hello." My response was shy, a schoolgirl's.

He extended his hand. I offered mine. He held it a few seconds longer than customary. Usually his handshake was over before you had felt his flesh next to your flesh. Like the practiced politician who knows how to keep the palms passing down the receiving line, he is adept at shaking off the sticky hands of transferring women. This handshake was both longer and more supple than usual.

"You look well," I said. His skin was browned, the gray hair at his temples silvered. I was aware of my own

manic state. We had to do something to get you out of it. You don't remember?"

"No. Nothing."

"You don't remember calling me when you got back from visiting your parents?"

"No."

"Most of the time you were manic, but when you called me you were sobbing. You were surprised at yourself. You said you didn't know you could still cry like that."

A stirring, somewhere in some deeply buried section of my mind, like a child wondering: Do I really remember doing that? Or do I just remember that they've told me I did it? "Maybe I remember. I'm not sure."

"You came by yourself. You were able to do that. You came in and you couldn't stop talking. You talked for two solid hours. You jumped around, acting things out; you gave marvelous imitations of people you'd seen at home—and"—a pause, a smile—"you were somewhat seductive."

"Oh?"

"Oh, not blatantly. You just didn't care where your skirt was. But I didn't mind: you know how lovely you are."

I returned his smile: one is supposed to acknowledge compliments. But inwardly I tensed. Why all these compliments? Because he feels sorry for me? Poor crazy girl. Tell her she's lovely. She can't be helped. Might as well make her feel good. Lies. Lies. They all lie to you.

In the hospital, Dr. Rosen, the others, they lied. They said I wouldn't have shock treatment and I did.

Abruptly again: "I called Dr. Rosen one day. I said, 'Am I psychotic?' He said, 'Absolutely not.' But how do I know he was telling the truth?"

"Do you trust me?" Compelling blue eyes, hypnotic. Our eyes meeting in a look that encompassed years. The room, the street sounds outside, his chair, my chair, their existence year after year, year after year of now loving him, now hating him, love, hate, the warp and woof of that look. Did I trust him? Of course. I allowed my silence to say yes for me.

"Then you will believe me when I say you are not psychotic?"

"All right. But what am I? What is a nervous breakdown?"

"There is no such thing, really, as a nervous breakdown."

"It's a euphemism?"

"Yes."

"Well, what did I have?"

"A psychotic episode."

Don't look at him. Look at the wall. The floor. Don't look at him until the words cease reverberating. Psychotic episode. That dreadful, terrifying word *psychotic* applied to *me!* When Clarence cracked up years ago, I laughed because Yvette said he had a "touch of schizophrenia." Psychotic episode. Is that "a touch of psychosis"?

"I've heard the term," I said finally, in a low voice.

"Then why did you make me spell it out?"

Another shrug.

"It was really quite mild, you know. A month is a short time for that sort of thing."

"Quite mild." Remember that he said that. Cherish it. Hope unfolded within me, like a Japanese paper flower unfolding in a glass of water. But a paper flower is not real. It's an illusion. A fake.

"But why did I have to have shock treatment, if it was mild? It's so difficult now. I can't remember so many things . . ."

"If you hadn't had shock treatment, it would have taken much longer . . . months. We tried drugs at first —but you didn't respond."

I don't remember. I don't remember. Horrible feeling of having been "done to," not *doing*. We tried this, we tried that . . . I don't remember. Where was I?

Silence in the room. Thundering in my brain. Wheels of a train, clacking out the same words over and over as the wheels go round and round: psychotic episode, psychotic episode, psychotic episode.

"How are you getting along at home?"

I looked out of the window of that train. My present life flashed by, while the wheels kept turning (psychotic episode, psychotic episode) : the children, Victoria, David, moving, seeing people, quick glimpses. How to describe this landscape?

"All right. The children are fine. But I'm still having

trouble remembering. I have so many things to do, because of moving, and I have to keep making lists so I won't forget what I have to do. Then I forget where I put the lists."

"Your memory will get better."

"Dr. Rosen said I would remember everything. But there are still so many blanks."

"You may never remember being in the hospital, but that doesn't matter. How is your husband?"

I fiddled with the binding on the upholstery of the chair. "Unnatural. Overly polite. He's kind of always tiptoeing around me. He pretends that everything is perfectly normal now, but he acts as though he were in a sickroom."

He smiled. "He came to see you every day, you know. I told him you wouldn't even remember if he'd been there, but he said he *had* to see you, see how you were. Of course, he can't act normally now; he's upset by what happened."

I remained silent for a long time.

"Yes, dear?" It was Dr. Stern's way of asking: What are you thinking about?

I looked at his solicitous expression for a moment and then said, "And you're the same way. You're being so careful! So kind!"

He laughed. "Just wait . . . it won't last. I'll have you hating me soon."

The chimes sounded. The next patient. I started to gather up my gloves and bag.

"You don't have to leave yet. Unless you want to. We have a few minutes."

Want to leave? Of course not. I realized that I had not asked what I had come prepared to ask.

"Why did it happen?"

He met my gaze, did not let his eyes swerve, did not brush aside my question: "I spent a lot of time thinking about you while I was on vacation. Many things contributed—two children so close together, your father's illness, other things—some we haven't talked about yet."

Words. Pat explanations. 'Anger sudden as a shock surged through me. "Oh, what does it matter? What good is theorizing? Why couldn't you prevent it? What good are you anyway?"

"See! I told you that you'd be hating me soon."

I subsided into sulkiness. "I'm in no mood for jokes."

"All right. I'll be very, very serious. You do remember that you hadn't been seeing me regularly for almost two years? There's so much I don't know about that period—"

"Oh, so now you're going to blame it on me! I should never have left you. I should have gone on forever dragging in here with the same old complaints—"

"I didn't say that. We'll talk about this next time I see you." He got up. "We'll have to stop now. I'm sorry."

Sorry! Insipid, ineffectual word! Despite his tan, he looked as gray as his words: a tired, middle-aged man, grown weak-eyed from his burrowing, subterranean, existence. I remembered with scorn the shy schoolgirl, eager to please, who had greeted him earlier. As he opened the door, I brushed by him; I could not wait to get away, to get back to light and air, even the soot-filled air of West End Avenue. I hailed a cab and told the driver to go through Central Park.

At dinner David, who through the years had scrupulously avoided showing any curiosity about my treatment, said, "What did Dr. Stern have to say?" Why did it happen? he meant but did not want to ask.

"Nothing much," I said and changed the subject.

The next day, as I cleaned out the hall closet, I came upon some old Valentines David had made me, along with poems and love letters we had written each other, dozens of photographs of me, photographs of us at our wedding, on our honeymoon, on vacation trips. Jammed into envelopes and broken cardboard boxes, those mementos were creased, wrinkled, tattered, torn, dusty, and dog-eared. They looked to me like artifacts of an ancient culture. Despite Dr. Rosen's advice, I could not keep my mind on the present then. I could not keep from slipping into the past. As I sorted my souvenirs and packed them into one large cardboard carton, I remembered the early days with David—and then the abrupt, inexplicable change.

Once I used to pace the floor of my apartment, dressed and ready too soon always, waiting for the sound of his footsteps, the exuberant slap of his hand against the wall as he took the stairs two at a time. Later, after we were married, it remained almost the same: I would sometimes, at a party, look at him across a room full of people and marvel that he was mine and find myself impatient to go home, to be alone with him again.

We were lovers then, but we were also partners. We both had full-time, demanding jobs, and when we were at home, he shared the chores with me. Some evenings he cooked dinner, some evenings I did. Some evenings we had no dinner but got up sleepily at midnight for sandwiches.

Until Larry was born. Suddenly, David was a different person. I should not have been surprised. He had been an only child in a fatherless home; he simply was not used to sharing. It is one thing to divide up the household chores; it is quite another matter to give up half, or more, of the attention you have been used to. I don't think he understood at all that he was jealous of Larry. And Beth, too, when she was born. He loved his children and was proud of them. But he wanted his wife to remain exactly as she had always been. It was impossible. Most of the time I was just plain tired.

I was tired of months without a night of sleep unbroken by a child's cries. Tired of entertaining friends until one or two in the morning and then getting up with babies at six. A good hostess, David insisted, did not excuse herself and go to bed. But it's rude of *them* to stay so long, I pleaded. So why can't I be rude, too? Sometimes I was: I did go to bed, but in the morning he would berate me for having done so. And I wished that he might get up some Saturday or Sunday morning so that for once I could get enough sleep.

When things got too bad at home, I would go to see Dr. Stern, who said on one occasion, "Why do you let him dominate you so? Run the household the way you want to. Why do you always rise to his bait?"

Because once he loved me when I felt unlovable, and once he telephoned me at three o'clock in the morning, when I lived alone in a cell of an apartment, to read to me Dylan Thomas' "Ballad of the Long-Legged Bait." It is a long poem; the only lines I have memorized are these: "For we saw him throw to the swift flood/ A girl alive with his hooks through her lips;/ All the fishes were rayed with blood,/ Amid the dwindling ships." That night he read the entire poem, and then said, "I love you, my long-legged bait." A girl alive with his hooks through her lips. Because once he loved me, his long-legged bait. Did he still love me? I did not know. He had been kind to me while I was in the hospital, but kindness is not love. And now that I was home? Strangers do not love one another. But they do not share a carton of keepsakes, either.

I had meant to wash my hair in the afternoon, but Maybelle called around noon and asked if she could come over. By the time she left, I didn't feel like starting in on the job, even though I don't like to wash my hair in the evening: a man shouldn't have to look at his wife in that kind of disarray, even a man who has been married for ten years.

It was a surprisingly cool evening for August. I came out of the bathroom with a thick green towel twisted into a turban around my head and carrying a clean comb, clean hairbrush, and a Kleenex box full of hair rollers and bobby pins. I would have gone into the bedroom to dry my hair and roll it up, to avoid getting water and hair all over the couch, but I knew that David did not like to sit alone in the evening. Especially after being alone for a month of evenings. I looked in on the children, saw that they were covered, then went in to David.

He was sitting in the orange chair, reading. "You'll ruin your eyes," I said. "Why don't you sit over on the couch by the light?" Sometimes when I hear myself talking I am aware that I sound exactly like my mother. She was always after us about sitting where the light was good. "You'll ruin your eyes!"—those were the very words she used. We never paid any attention to her, but perhaps she was right. All three of us now need glasses for reading. David, too, ignored the admonition.

As I put my paraphernalia down on the couch, I was shivering. There was too much breeze: the bamboo shades were flapping against the sills. The building we lived in was an old one, poorly kept up. The windows were so thickly encrusted with paint that I could not raise or lower them without great effort. Usually I just asked David to do it.

I didn't even have to ask him. He looked up and

said, "Too much breeze? You look very exotic in that turban."

He got up and lowered the windows. I pulled the towel from my hair. It hung in wet, tangled hanks. Some of it flopped over my forehead.

David collapsed into the orange chair and laughed at me. "God! You should see yourself."

"I'm fully aware of what I look like when I dry my hair. Don't look if it's so awful. Read your book."

"I don't feel like reading now."

"Well, then go and watch television."

"I'd rather watch you."

"So you can laugh?"

"You know I think you're lovely—even with wet hair."

I crossed my legs. My robe fell open almost to my waist. I had nothing on beneath the robe. A deliberate action? Perhaps.

"And you have the greatest legs in the world."

"*Had,* maybe. Before the children."

I picked up the towel and began rubbing my hair vigorously with it. The room felt warmer, but I wished that we had a fireplace. It was too warm for a fire, even if we had had a fireplace, but I wanted to sit before a fire and dry my hair and listen to David's compliments, as soothing and familiar as a child's favorite bedtime tale.

A crackle of static disturbed my fantasy. David got up and changed the station: cool jazz was replaced by Handel's *Water Music*. He sat down again, but after a few

back, I don't think I want it. I had the foolish notion
that this would never have happened if I had dried my
hair in the bedroom.

"Well, there isn't really very much to tell. You got
pregnant. It was a mistake. You were very depressed.
Three babies in three years. . . . you were having all
that trouble with your back, too, and you kept saying
you didn't want to have an unwanted child. You don't
remember any of this?"

"No." I put the comb down on the coffee table beside me. Then I picked it up again and ran my finger up
and down the tips of the teeth. I felt enormously interested in that comb. The teeth at one end of the comb
were shorter and thinner and set closer together than
the teeth in the other section.

"Are you *trying* to remember?"

I looked up at him. "Why, of course."

"You don't even seem to be listening."

"I heard every word you said." I didn't tell him that
it was a radio voice I heard, talking about a make-believe
person in a make-believe play. He kept saying "you,"
but if I were the "you," he would not have to be telling
me what happened; I would know. I've never liked listening to the radio. "Go on," I said, to be polite.

"You asked Dr. Stern to help you. You thought maybe
it could be done legally, in a hospital, for psychiatric
reasons. But he said no, you weren't sick enough or something. So we had to start asking friends. First John and
Harriet, but you didn't like the way their man sounded,

then I think you called Peggy and she was supposed to get a name for you, but Maybelle came up with this guy . . ."

All these people knew more about what had happened than I did! I could remember nothing. Or could I? "How did *you* feel about it?" I asked. "You keep saying what I did. But what about you? I mean, what were you doing? Did you want the baby?"

He looked startled. "I? Why, I told you it was entirely up to you. Whatever you wanted to do was all right with me."

So it was all up to me, and that is what I had done. I had killed my third child. Conversation ended as I sat contemplating my burden of guilt. We both returned to private worlds.

As far back as I can remember, I can hear my mother saying it: "You were a little mistake." I heard it so often it almost seemed like a nickname. Little Mistake —like Little Miss Muffet or Little Red Riding Hood. My mother smiled at me as she said it. She has a small mouth, but her front teeth are large and her gums show when she smiles. She is not a large woman, but I was just a child then, when she smiled at me and said, "You were a little mistake," and I knew I was supposed to smile back at her, but I didn't feel like smiling. I wanted to run away and hide, to curl up in some cozy dream corner where there were no spiders, no wolves masquerading as Grandma and no mothers who smiled enormously and showed their large front teeth and pink gums and said, "Mistake!"

"Of course, we loved you after you were born," she always added each time she said, "You were a little mistake." But I knew that loving me was something she had no choice about. She had to love me because I was her child, just as I had to love her because she was my mother. I had to, even though sometimes she frightened me.

"And if we *had* wanted a third child, we would certainly have wanted a boy, not another girl. We had your name all picked out: Ralph Stuart Wolfe. Stuart, after your real uncle; Ralph, for Daddy's good friend, Uncle Ralph. We never even thought about what we'd name a girl. Everyone was so sure we'd have a boy . . . and then *you* came along."

That then was my original sin, being born at all. I never even got a chance at the apple. My doom, like the afterbirth, followed me into the world.

"David told me the other day that I had an abortion. I can't remember it at all. Usually when he tells me about something that has happened, then I remember."

Dr. Stern looked at me for a moment before he answered. His kindness seemed almost palpable, as visible as dust motes suspended in sunshine. "Perhaps it is harder for you to recover the memories that are most painful."

"It was a bad experience, then?"

"Oh, you were very pleased with the doctor. He was actually an obstetrician. Very well qualified. And you liked his manner very much."

"That doesn't sound very painful."

"I'm convinced it was the major factor in your breakdown."

I didn't say anything for a while. It is hard to talk about something you do not remember.

He broke the silence for me. "Do you remember when I visited you in the hospital?"

"No! You came to see me! I don't remember!"

He groaned. "Three times I come to see you and you don't even remember! Why, I even held your hand!"

I smiled. "Goodness, how could I forget an event like that? Why did you do it?"

"Oh, we were walking down the hall and I suddenly felt like holding your hand, so I did."

"That doesn't sound like very orthodox behavior."

"You know I'm not a very orthodox psychiatrist."

He looked relaxed and confident, leaning back in his leather chair. He wore his gray hair in a crew cut so that his growing baldness would not be so noticeable. I suddenly felt irritated with him. What right had he to look so smug? He had been treating me for years, before either of us had any gray hair, yet I had had a breakdown. "Not a very good psychiatrist, either," I said.

His face immediately grew serious. "Why do you say that? Because you had a breakdown? It's true that I've had some guilt feelings about it. I know you feel that

your treatment has not been as successful as it might
have been, but I think the major factor in your breakdown was the abortion. The trip home was important,
but the abortion was more traumatic than seeing your
family again."

Of course he would choose to absolve himself from
blame. His ego is large, at times infuriatingly so. I
thought that if I were in his place, I would feel that my
work was useless. But he went on seeing his patients and
collecting fees and playing chess and sailing his boat.

He has a way of lifting his chin and turning his head,
as though toward an outside sound, when a thought occurs to him. "You don't remember what you said to
me, then, in the hospital?" He waited, his head still
turned to the left, for my answer.

"I told you, I don't remember your visits at all."

"You said, 'If you were a third, unwanted child and
you kill your own third, unwanted child, does that
mean that you don't have to kill yourself?' "

I was there in his office, but at the same time I was a
small child, sitting on the cold, blue linoleum floor, at
my mother's feet, hearing again the smiling words I
hated: "You were a little mistake." Then I was lying on
my bed, late at night, with David's arms around me; I
was sobbing into a pillow, "I won't have an unwanted
child. I won't have a 'mistake,' I won't, I won't!" His
voice, always so conciliatory: "Everything will be all
right, you'll see. We'll find a doctor." The tense days of
surreptitious talks with friends who, I came to feel, were

enjoying my predicament: at least it gave them something to talk about at dinner time. I imagined I could hear them saying, "How could she be so careless! Three babies in three years!"

I knew right away that I was pregnant. It wasn't more than a few days after the conception that I *knew*. I was getting dressed one morning; I was hooking my brassiere, and suddenly I knew that my breasts were the breasts of a pregnant woman. David was lying in bed. "I'm pregnant," I said.

He yawned. "You're always thinking that."

"That was before I ever had a baby. And I wanted one. But now I know what it feels like. I'm pregnant! I know it. I don't want another baby! I can't take care of *three* babies! I can't! It's too much!"

"Will you for God's sake not get all hysterical until you know whether you really *are* pregnant?"

At that moment, I hated him. Hated him for lying in that warm bed, looking so relaxed and confident. His body would never bulge with unwanted life . . .

"So?" Dr. Stern's voice: a hand shaking me out of a nightmare.

"David didn't believe me when I told him I was pregnant. He always says I worry too much. But I really *had* something to worry about."

"Of course you did," he said gently. "The two of you were equally to blame for the conception—yet you were the one who had the abortion. You were the one who had to make the decision."

"Yes," I said. I felt exhausted, old, spent. I remembered a favorite expression of my mother's: old as the hills. That was how I felt: old as the hills. Barren hills, with a cold wind whistling over them. Black storm clouds heavy in the sky. Not a house or a human soul in sight.

"What are you thinking?"

"I'm not really thinking. I'm just looking at a picture in my mind—it's a bleak landscape, funereal . . ."

"Whose funeral is it? Is it yours?"

"Why, no." Then, without thinking, I allowed myself to say what he perhaps knew I would say: "It's my child's. My third child, the unwanted one. The one I killed."

Suddenly I was sobbing. "Why did you let me do it? Why? Why didn't you know what would happen?"

He looked troubled. "We . . . we all thought it would be best for you."

"But why didn't you *know*?"

He did not answer. I did not blame him.

Later, another letter from Mother. She was so glad to hear from me finally. They still could not understand how I could let a month go by without writing to them. She was glad to hear that we were all well and that we would be moving soon, as she was sure the children would love the country. Daddy was the same. They both enjoyed a dish of ice cream every afternoon.

The final paragraph began with "Dear," and before I read it I tensed with apprehension because whenever she begins a paragraph in this manner, it concerns some social duty that I have neglected: "Dear, you really ought to write your Aunt Selma. After all, she is all alone in the world and does not have a husband and two lovely children to keep her company." Or, "Dear, your sister Sara tells me that you have not been to see her in weeks. You know they all love to see you so why don't you take your family out there soon?"

My apprehension was well founded. This time she wrote: "Dear, I spoke to Patricia today and was astonished to learn that neither she or Carol have heard from you since you returned to New York. Why have you waited so long to write and thank them?"

Thank them for what? Patricia I did at least remember seeing. We had gone someplace together one evening, to an old plantation that is now an inn, I vaguely remembered. She had driven my father and mother and me to the doctor's office for his checkup. It was possible that she had also driven me to the airport; I had no clear picture of the return trip. But what else had she done for me? I had been to her house. That much I was sure of. But whether it was for a luncheon or a cocktail party or a dinner party or merely a quiet visit I could not say.

The only event I remembered with any clarity was a luncheon, the gathering of many of the "girls" I had gone to high school with, all of us well into our thirties by that time. Some of the women seemed remarkably like the girls they had been, with clear, unlined skin,

good figures, hair untouched by gray. Others had
frankly given up, grown comfortably fat. Still others
looked old because they dressed like matrons, in a manner astonishingly similar to my mother's style of dress.
Their dowdy, demurely flowered dresses, discreetly cov-
ering their kneecaps, their nondescript straw hats, their
clean white gloves and polished, low-heeled white
pumps seemed right for them. They looked like women
who were comfortable with their role in life; they felt
no need to compete or strive for eternal youth.

The dowdy ones were not among the eight or ten
of us who, after a lengthy luncheon, adjourned to a near-
by bar for mint juleps and still later had cocktails together beside the pool of one of the wealthier women. It
was a haphazard, drunken afternoon. I think someone
jumped into the pool with her clothes on. Or was there
just talk of it? I don't remember. Various husbands
drifted in and out of the picture, were sent away to
pick up children, to fetch chocolate eclairs, to stop by a
cleaner's for clothes urgently needed. I had forgotten
the docility of Southern men: all of the husbands did
as they were told, without a murmur of protest, while
the wives laughed and drank and reminisced about the
crazy teachers we had had, the silly things we had done.
("Remember the time I didn't go to Spanish for a
month because I said I was rehearsing for the *Invisible
Choir* in the Christmas pageant? It was invisible, all
right!" "Remember when Babcock ate all the cookies

that were props in the class play? And Riley had to pass an empty plate during the performance?") I found it disconcerting that they still addressed each other by their maiden names, in boarding-school style.

They made rather a fuss over me, however, because I was now the outsider. The swimming pool group met regularly; it was no reunion for them. They were linked by marriages as well, and sometimes I could not follow their talk when it left the past and ambled into the present. Now just who is Maurice? I would wonder. Her husband? Her brother? Her brother-in-law? They took it for granted that all of the names they threw out meant something to me. I felt both at home with them and sharply alienated from them, especially when they questioned me about my life up North. "Ellen, honey, do you have many colored friends? I know you Northerners are just *crazy* about Nigras," one woman, an avid segregationist, said to me. Only the fact that she had been extremely kind to my mother since my father's illness kept my reply mild. "I don't have many Negro friends," I said. "Just a few." She had expected an argument. My simple reply silenced her.

It's my impression that this luncheon was the day after I arrived. Perhaps that's why I remember it, but only bits and pieces of other social events. I don't know whether one goes abruptly or gradually into a manic state, but I believe that it was sometime *during* that visit, rather than after I returned, that I slipped into it. Why

no one seemed to notice, I cannot say. Perhaps Southerners are more used to, more tolerant of, eccentric behavior.

I did wonder, however, how I had behaved at all those
parties. But perhaps there had been only one and my
memory was shattering it into shards. Somewhere there
had been lots of people crowded into a living room,
drinking, laughing, talking about old times. Who had
been the hostess? Patricia, probably, and Mother's letter seemed to indicate that Carol too had entertained
me. But I could not even remember seeing Carol while
I was home. Sometime previously, this absence of any
recollection of Carol had occurred to me and I had puzzled over it.

"Did I see Carol while I was home?" I asked David.

"Now, let's see, which one is she?"

"Oh, David," I said impatiently. "You've met her.
Very blond and skinny and nervous. Always joking."

"Oh, yes," he said vaguely.

"Well, did I see her? I don't seem to remember, but I
can't figure out why I wouldn't have unless she was
out of town. After all, she was one of my best friends."

"Honey, I'm sorry, but I just don't remember. You
talked so much when you got back, and I just couldn't
keep everything straight."

Evidently she had not been away and I had seen her.
Her children, too, I suppose, and her new house, which
I had not seen before. Because I still needed my
mother's approval, I would have liked to have gone right

to my desk then and composed charming thank-you notes to Patricia and Carol so that they would tell Mother, "Oh, we got the most delightful letter from Ellen!" Obviously, this was impossible. How can you write a "charming" thank-you note devoid of any specific reference? "Dear Carol: Thank you so much for your hospitality. I enjoyed seeing you." That would never do. I had to remain silent and let them think that now that I am a Yankee, I no longer have any manners.

I decided not to tell David about Mother's letter. It was merely another of those niggling annoyances that kept springing up like weeds each day.

One morning I looked through my appointment book ("Venice Views and Echoes," published by the Metropolitan Museum of Art) in an attempt to recover something of the days that were lost to me. On the page opposite a reproduction of a painting by Canaletto, I found an entry that transfixed me: *Dr. Levine. 2 o'clock.* How innocent it looked. It was written in the same casual hand I had used to jot down the names of the baby-sitters I had hired for the Friday and Saturday nights following that Tuesday. *Dr. Levine. 2 o'clock.* It was not written any larger than the other two entries. It was not underlined or starred or written in red. I was swept by a wave of nausea almost like morning sickness as I sat at my desk, staring at a name written in my appointment book, because just seeing it brought back, if not the

whole, more fragments of the abortion than I felt I
could contain in my bruised mind.

My first call to his office, terrified, wondering what
to say if the nurse asked, "Why do you want to see the
doctor?" Mercifully, she did not, merely made an appointment for me, in a businesslike voice. Seeing him
in his office, the door closed between him and the nurse's
desk. Wondering: Does she know what goes on? Of
course she must. The doctor, a tall, slim, elderly man
with gray hair and a natural dignity. "Are you sure you
want to do this, my dear? I can assure you that you have
nothing to worry about—there is absolutely no danger
—but are you really sure in your own heart that this is
what you want to do?"

I was sure, I told him, not at all sure that it was so.

"The fee will be seven hundred and fifty dollars."

More than I expected, but it did not matter to me
what it cost. I thought, not of the money, but of the one
photograph I have ever seen of myself as a baby. I am
sitting in a carriage screened with mosquito netting. I
am wearing an elaborately smocked white dress and a
lace-trimmed bonnet, but on my face is a look of painful
bewilderment. No, I did not want a child like that.

"There will be some pain—not a great deal. I don't
give anesthesia because I need your help."

Pain. Why did he have to tell me that so far in advance?
My mind could imagine more pain than hell could
dream of. And I didn't believe him—he didn't want to
give me anesthesia because it increased the danger.

He smiled at me. "Are you a brave girl?"

"No, not particularly."

He smiled again. "Oh, I'm sure you are. Just trust me and do as I say and everything will be all right. Bring the money when you come—in cash."

At the door, as though embarrassed to have ended on this commercial note, he said, in a paternal tone, concern, compassion, tinged with disapproval, all smoothly blended into a richly professional voice: "If you change your mind, my dear, don't hesitate to call and tell me so."

I thanked him and went home to wait . . . how long? Two, perhaps three, days. Endless days. Almost as tense as the days when I was still wondering what to do. Then the day itself, ironically clear and beautiful. No pathetic fallacies in this story! Victoria came in earlier so that I could be there by two. "I'll need you earlier," I had told her. "I have to go to the doctor." Victoria. She was well named. My father sang "Rule, Britannia," but the empire no longer ruled, and brown-skinned Victoria held my small world together as I was led away in chains.

David came home too early. He paced around in the living room while the children napped and Victoria washed the lunch dishes. And I got myself ready. I didn't want to wear black: black would be too appropriate. But in the end I did put on my black knit suit, because everything else was wrinkled or too warm for the mild weather or at the cleaner's. A voice like a recording said to me as I put on my liquid makeup and lipstick and eyebrow pencil: I am getting ready to go have an abortion. I may die on the operating table because he does not have the proper equipment or I may have to be rushed to the hospital in the middle of the operation or I may be arrested.

It is illegal to have an abortion.

I have never violated a criminal law. I don't even jaywalk very often.

I seldom lie.

I am known as an honest woman.

If I am, it is because of my father.

Daddy doesn't lie or cheat or steal or break laws—ever.

What would Daddy say if he knew what I was doing?

He would condemn me. For I am a criminal.

By definition, a criminal is one who commits a crime. It doesn't matter whether you get caught or not. Get caught. An unfortunate choice of words. I got caught, all right . . .

David's voice from the living room: "Aren't you ready yet? What are you doing, for God's sake?"

Nothing, for *God's* sake. I am doing this for *my* sake. My voice, answering him, matched his in irritation: "I'll be ready in a minute. Why did you have to come home so soon?"

He didn't answer. Beth whimpered as though she were awakening and then was silent again. How quiet it seems at midday when the children are asleep.

I stood before him in the living room. "I'm ready."

"Did you tell Victoria we were leaving?"

"Oh, I forgot."

"I'll do it."

"No, no, I want to." I poked my head into the kitchen and said with more tenderness than I had intended: "Good-bye, Victoria." I could not bear to say the usual "See you later." Later it would be all over. Victoria, take good care of my children while I am gone. They are so little! Watch them carefully. Don't let anything harm them. Please, God, I don't believe in you, but if you do exist, and if you're going to punish me, don't use my children as the weapon . . .

In the taxi we rode in silence. Once David said, "If I could, I would change places with you. Gladly. You know that, don't you?"

"I suppose," I said. I guess he expected me to smile bravely at him, but I didn't. Words. What did they mean? Nothing at all. He knew he could not change places with me. I hated him: he was male, exempt forever from this kind of misery.

What else did I remember?

Some preparations—I suppose the nurse shaved me. And pain.

Rather less than I had expected. It was no worse than mild labor pains or bad menstrual cramps.

I was a brave girl, after all. I didn't cry out. I moaned a little. I lay still when he told me to.

Very soon it was all over. I dressed. David handed the money to the doctor. He asked me to come in the following week so that he could check on my condition. "And bring your diaphragm," he said. "I want to make sure it's properly fitted. I don't want you showing up here again in six months or so." I said I would and thank you very much. We went home and drank two martinis and broiled a steak and lived happily ever after.

"I must say, you took the whole thing very well," David said a few weeks later.

I said, "It's strange, but I really feel very unemotional about it now. It's almost as though it never happened."

I would have done better to wail like the women of Troy.

Shortly before we were to move, David presented me with a sheet of paper torn from his address book. On it he'd listed five moving companies. Beside each name he'd printed the time of an appointment.

"Look," he said, "I've called all these companies and made the appointments. All you have to do is to be here when they come, and over here I've left space for you to write down the estimate each one gives you. Is that clear?"

I put the list down on the coffee table and took a sip of my tea. Too much sugar in it. "Of course it's clear."

"You won't forget and go out when they're coming?"

"Why should I?"

"Sometimes you forget things."

"You know I'm much better now."

He was pacing up and down in the living room. He picked up the list. "Where do you want to keep this?"

"Oh, just leave it there on the coffee table. I'll put it away later."

"I'd rather you did it now."

I sighed, then banged my teacup down on the brass tray so that it made an enormous clatter. I made a big production out of wearily getting up from the couch. If he is going to treat me like an invalid, I might as well act like one, I thought. I took the paper from him and went back to my desk in the bedroom. After I had slipped the list into my appointment book, I sat down at my desk for a while.

I didn't like the way David was handling the business of moving. Why couldn't he have asked me to call the companies and make the appointments? Isn't that what he would have done ordinarily, "before"? With Victoria in the house all day, I had time on my hands. His attempts to "spare" me were insulting—more than that, debilitating. If he expected that I could do very little, I would be able to do very little.

But I should not be angry with him, I thought. He has been very patient with me. It is myself I am angry with. I do not want to be an invalid wife.

I turned off the light in the bedroom and went back to find David. We watched television together. I pretended that I wanted to see the movie and gave an excellent imitation of enjoying it.

*   *   *

One day, alone in the apartment, tired of packing and sorting, I sat down at my desk and wrote the following:

"Thou shalt not kill." Most of us who have broken away from the religious training of our childhood do not question the validity of this commandment. Many people commit adultery without crushing themselves with guilt. We certainly fail to remember the Sabbath Day and keep it holy. We take the Lord's name in vain at the slightest provocation (Christ! Is it raining again?). We do not honor our mother and father. In fact, it is quite chic to sit around at cocktail parties smashing their images. But we do not condone murder.

A number of my friends are pacifists. Two were conscientious objectors during the last war. Several belong to peace groups and we all agree the bomb should be banned.

But what of feticide? If I have a right to prevent David's sperm from joining with my ova, have I the right to banish a fetus from my womb? My intellect says yes, but my heart says no, you are a murderer.

Christianity gave the embryo a soul. Exactly when the soul entered the embryo was a subject for ecclesiastical debate during the early days of the Church. Today, the Catholic Church still holds that the mother must be sacrificed if the infant can thereby be saved, because the mother has been baptized and can therefore go to heaven but the fetus would remain in limbo forever.

As a child, I was surrounded by Catholics, although I

was not one. Teachers, friends, neighbors, almost all were Catholics. Did some of their beliefs permeate my unconscious? What else contributed to the formation of my feelings against abortion? I cannot say for sure. My parents, good Victorians, never discussed the subject. But this very lack of mention must have created in me the conviction that abortion is unspeakably evil.

I am not at all sure what the "soul" of man is, yet, like St. Augustine, I find myself pondering the question: When does the embryo acquire a "soul"? Even if it were a simple matter medically, I would not be able to submit to the abortion of a fetus close to term. By then, it already seems a "baby." Where does my morality draw the line? After quickening? I can produce no logic to support this view. It seems as arbitrary as St. Thomas' decision for the time of animation: the fortieth day for males, the eightieth day for females. But perhaps he did have some reasons. I don't know anything about St. Thomas, except what I learned from Simone de Beauvoir in her book *The Second Sex*.

Feticide. That is the word we use for the act of abortion. In man, the embryo becomes a fetus after the third month, according to my dictionary. May I conclude then that disposing of the embryo before the third month is a lesser crime?

I must organize my thoughts; they ramble. I must remember these things: I am not a Catholic. Their views cannot touch me. I do not believe that it is morally wrong to have an abortion.

This inescapable fact remains, however: I committed a crime. The law is the law, as the saying goes. I would not condemn a friend for breaking the law, but I condemn myself. I cannot rid myself of the feeling that something terrible will happen to Beth as retribution. I have no fears for my son. It is my daughter who will be punished. In my most depressed moments, I think that she will have to die because I killed my unborn child. Primitive morality: an eye for an eye.

"What nonsense," I can say now about my thoughts of five years ago. Since that time, in many states, organized pressure groups have been seeking to change the stringent abortion laws of this country. Almost every major consumer magazine has carried articles on "the abortion question." At least one state has actually passed legislation liberalizing its abortion law. I sometimes wonder if I would have avoided a breakdown had the abortion been done legally, for psychiatric reasons. I am inclined to doubt it. My own personal morality cannot be altered by legislation.

In any case, the number of women who require or desire abortions must surely have diminished in the past five years: most of us now take the Pill. Even five years ago, vast numbers of women were already taking it. I, however, had a conservative doctor: "Wait," he said. "I want to know more about the side effects before I prescribe it for you. Maybe next year . . ." Two years later, another doctor gave me a prescription for the Pill and I have taken it ever since, with no trouble at all. If my

first doctor had been less conservative . . . but there
is no point in sitting around thinking "if only."

A few days after my attempt at an essay on abortion, I
received another letter from Mother. Daddy could no
longer hear at all, she reported. She had to write down
everything she said to him. She took him to an ear doctor and the doctor removed a big plug of wax, but it
didn't help. He still enjoyed a dish of ice cream in the
evening.

I sat on the living room couch holding the letter and
let the tears run down my face. Down the hall, in Larry's
room, the children were making a terrible racket:
screeching, screaming, banging toys about. I can't stand
all this noise, I thought, and then my tears, which had
ceased, began again. I wondered if Daddy still spoke to
Mother. Surely he must, I decided. I tried to imagine
what it would be like to speak but hear no sound, neither your own voice nor an answering one. I had a picture in my mind of him sitting in a rocking chair, perfectly still and silent, while my mother, voluble as ever,
circled and recircled his chair in a frenzy of frustration.

Larry ran in and dumped a truck into my lap. "Mama
crying!" he said. He was dressed to go out; one shoe-
lace was already untied. "See!" He poked a finger in
my eye and grinned at me.

Victoria came in carrying Beth. Beth waved to me
and opened and closed her mouth in an attempt at
"Bye-bye." Sometimes it came out loud and lusty; other

times the sounds she made were so faint you could barely
hear them across the room. Was it because she lacked
the judgment to control her voice, or did she choose to
vary it in this way? Victoria, discreet as always, pretended
not to notice my tears. She took the children off to the
park and left me alone in the silent apartment.

One morning I worked very hard at packing. In the
afternoon, because it rained and Victoria could not take
the children out, I helped her amuse them: I built tow-
ers of blocks for Larry and made funny faces at Beth and
tickled her and taught her to say "belly button." Right
after dinner, the Jaffees came by for a drink. Because
my day was thus unusually crowded, I did not read the
morning paper until late in the evening. I stretched out
on the bed to read it, waiting for David, who was having
a snack, to come to bed.

The usual sort of news. A city official accused of graft.
Trouble in the Middle East. A Park Avenue landmark to
be razed. A new Italian film with Marcello Mastroianni.
Nothing arrested me for more than a few moments until I reached the last page of the first section: the obituary page. PERCY STERN, 67, TEACHER, SOCIAL WORKER, I
read.

Percy Stern. My gaze remained fixed on the headline
for the few seconds that it took for my mind to decide
that Percy Stern was a familiar name.

Percy Stern. But of course. Percy Stern was *his* father,

Dr. Stern's father. I skipped down to the last paragraph, customarily reserved for the listing of survivors. Yes, there was his name: Dr. Seymour B. Stern. The B. stood for Bysshe. Years ago I asked him why he always used a middle initial and what it stood for. I don't remember that he offered any explanation for his habit of including a middle initial in his signature (it seemed to me pretentious), but he did tell me that the B. was for Bysshe, his father's middle name.

I went back to the beginning of the article and read it through. For a man who had been only a minor success, it was impressively long, almost a half column. He had obviously been a man of some ability, a person useful to and interested in the society in which he lived. But I wondered what kind of father he had been and how his death would affect Dr. Stern.

It seemed sadly ironic to me that my own father, before whose transience I had trembled for years, should outlive his father, who was many years younger.

But in a way, my father had not outlived him. When I told Dr. Stern that I dreaded having to attend my father's funeral, because I was afraid I might crack up again, he said: "I don't think you need worry about that. In your mind he is already dead—and has been for many months. You have already experienced his death." I remembered then a line from a poem by Dylan Thomas: "After the first death, there is no other."

That spring, my very old father and my very young child both died. If after the first death, there is no other,

I did not need to mourn the death of my very young
child. It is sentimental to call a five-week-old embryo a
child. Yet sometimes I couldn't help wondering what
color my child's eyes would have been and whether my
child would have been tall or short, bright or dull, gifted
or ordinary. It is sentimental also to mourn, pre-
maturely or otherwise, the death of a very old man. Yet
I could not help despairing that my children would not
know their grandfather. Percy Stern knew his grand-
children. How old were Dr. Stern's children then? Eight
and ten. No, older, I think. Perhaps ten and twelve. Like
me, he has a boy and a girl. The boy first, then the girl.
How neat. How nice. The perfect American family. He
himself was an only child. He never had to fight for a
chance at his father's lap.

When David came into the bedroom, smelling of pea-
nut butter, seeming more like a son than a husband, he
found me clipping out the obituary with my manicure
scissors.

"What are you doing?" he asked.

"Dr. Stern's father died."

"Let me see."

He read the notice and handed it back. "Why are you
saving it?"

"I don't know."

He smiled, a bit ruefully. "How like you."

I think he had intended to make love to me, but re-
spectful of my preoccupation, he did not approach me.

*   *   *

My daughter's first birthday. Did David have to tell me of its approach or did I remember it by myself? I don't know. Probably he had to tell me. It fell on a Sunday. The day before, I went down to Lord and Taylor's and bought her a yellow and white checked jumper and a set of colorful foam rubber blocks. I had intended to get more presents, but the Saturday afternoon crowds in the store bothered me: to get a clerk's attention required an aggressiveness I did not then possess. When I got home I showed David the things I had bought for her and said, "I don't know. It doesn't seem enough. I feel as though I should *celebrate* her birthday."

"She's only a year old," David said. "She won't know the difference."

"But we ought to do *something*."

"We are doing something. We're going to the Greens' in the afternoon—with the children. Don't you remember?"

How tired I was of that question. How tired I was of forgetting, over and over again forgetting. "Oh, yes," I said, lying, to reassure him.

The next day, after their naps, I dressed Beth in her new jumper and Larry in some shorts of the same pattern, with a new white top, and we took them over to the Greens'. They lived only a few blocks away, in a new building, on a high floor that provides a splendid view of the city. Jim is a tall, quiet, pipe-smoking man who still speaks with a trace of a Southern accent. Elaine is a bouncy brunette, an efficient, intelligent woman from the Midwest.

They welcomed us warmly into their apartment, yet I felt somewhat awkward, as I did when seeing anyone for the first time after that month away. I always felt that people must be on the lookout for signs of strangeness in me. But if Jim and Elaine were, they concealed it well. Elaine led the children back to her daughter's room to play, while David and I settled down on a couch, and Jim opened a bottle of wine. When Elaine returned, he poured the wine and handed us each a glass.

"Let's drink to Beth," I said. "It's her birthday today."

Jim and Elaine exchanged smiles. "I know," Elaine said. "I have it written down."

"Wonderful wine," David said, but Elaine and Jim had already put down their glasses.

"Come," Elaine said, so David and Jim and I followed her down the hall. Tacked onto the door of their daughter's room was a large sign, carefully lettered: HAPPY BIRTHDAY, BETH. Elaine pushed open the door and I saw a scene set for a party: balloons, streamers, blowers, a small pile of presents. My eyes filled with tears. I was touched by Elaine's thoughtfulness but ashamed that she had done what I should have done. We had our celebration. Beth puffed at the two candles (one to grow on), but did not manage to blow them out, and explored the icing, while Jim recorded the scene with his Polaroid, and David and I sipped our wine, and Larry tried to accept his secondary role. (Why all this fuss over a baby? he obviously thought.)

I was grateful to the Greens. It is good to have friends. Yet I could not help feeling that it was a celebration I should have created. I did not like my role of contrite convalescent.

My sister Martha called to say that she would be in town that day and did I want to have lunch?

"Why don't you come over here about one?" I said. "The children will be asleep then."

"Oh, no," she said, sounding almost shocked at the suggestion. "I don't want to tire you. We'll go to a restaurant."

Tire me? Just how fragile did she think I was? "Oh, I'll just fix sandwiches and a salad. And I have Victoria all day, you know, for the children."

"No," she said, in the firm voice she uses with her children. "What's a restaurant near you?"

We arranged to meet at a place on Third Avenue. Knowing that she thought me still so unsteady as to be tired out by spreading mustard on bread had an unnerving effect on me. On the way to meet her, I forced a briskness I did not feel into my walk. I waved when I caught sight of her standing in front of the restaurant and called out a cheerful hello. She raised a white-gloved hand in salute but did not speak until I was at her side. She looked lovely, as usual, her soft blond hair recently "done," her blue linen suit fresh from the cleaner's, on the lapel, a silver pin—from Tiffany's, no doubt.

Martha is the pretty one in our family: my sister Sara and I both freely acknowledge this, which embarrasses Martha. She knows she is pretty—in a proper, Grace Kelly kind of way—but she has never chosen to use, or perhaps never known how to use, her good looks in a manipulative manner. She lives rather by her intelligence. Sara says Martha has a masculine mind because she reads books in the fields of politics, history, and sociology that Sara and I would never get through. I think her reading takes that direction because she is married to an economist. Married to a poet, she would read poetry. Married to an artist, she would take up ceramics and wear Mexican dresses.

But it is difficult to imagine Martha married to an artist. Or a poet. She seems right as she is: the wife of a successful professional man who belongs to the Yale Club and is willing to go to church with her (she is the only one of us still an Episcopalian), living in an attractive Colonial house in Westchester, with her three handsome, healthy, blond children. She does not like being known as the conventional one of the sisters, but she does not dislike her life. In fact, she is puzzled by my restlessness.

The restaurant was one of those Third Avenue places that are meant to look like English pubs. Lots of dark wood paneling. A turn-of-the-century bar. Brass fixtures holding large round bulbs. At night, crowded with

about God and death. How are you going to explain death to a child if you don't bring in religion?" She did not wait for an answer, but silently I did answer her. How indeed? I said. How explain death to anyone? The answer is, it can't be explained, only experienced. And "after the first death, there is no other." In the middle of Martha's monologue, the waiter brought our hamburgers and, incredibly, a cup of coffee for me. He slammed it down in front of me, sloshing some into the saucer.

"Look," I said, controlled fury in my voice, "I told you twice, quite clearly and politely, I do not want my coffee with my meal!"

I could feel Martha stiffen with disapproval. She would never make a scene in public, a martyr to marriage and matronage. I could hear her telling her husband that evening, "Honestly, you can't imagine what a scene she made over a cup of coffee. She was furious with the waiter and I was really embarrassed, the way she talked to him. If that's what going to a psychiatrist does for you, I'm glad *I* never went to one." I don't usually go around making scenes in restaurants, but looking back on this episode, I realize that the fact that I *could* get angry at the waiter was an indication that I was recovering; my sleepwalking was over.

The waiter took the coffee away. To spite me, to challenge me, he brought the check a few minutes later: I was not to have coffee after my meal, he had decided. I let it pass. My mind was on other things. Martha had just asked, as always, "Have you heard from Mother

lately?" Before I could answer, she rushed on: "I had a
letter a couple of days ago and she sounded fine. She
seems to be managing quite well."

I remembered then, as Martha talked on, an incident
that Dr. Stern had recalled to me on a recent visit to
him. So intense was the memory that as I visualized it,
it seemed actually to recur: My mother, hysterical on
the street in front of our house, cowering in fright,
pointing to the open front door, shrilly crying: "There's
someone in the house! Don't go in! I closed the door
when I left, I locked it, there's someone in there!" My
father, blindly, weakly, stumbling up the steep front
stairs. Exhausted by his trip to the doctor's office, he was
frantic to reach his familiar, sagging couch, to lie down
again, to sleep, to rest, or die. And I, caught between
them in that moment, wavered on the sidewalk. My father needed my arm at his elbow: he might easily slip,
fall, break a hip or leg. My mother needed me. She was
frozen there on the sidewalk in a weird, half-crouching
position, now screaming, "Police! Police! Call the police!"

It was a moment as horrible as any nightmare. The
strong sun burned my hair. The sky was blue and empty.
There was no breeze. There were no cars on the street;
there were no strollers on the sidewalk; there were no
women rocking on porches. I stood there forever, in
an agony of indecision, caught up in my mother's fear:
was there really someone in the house? A man, ruthless,

desperate, who might turn on us in a rage because he had found nothing of value in the house?

My father stumbled on the stairs. I had to follow, had to race after him, put out a guiding hand. He did not comment on the open door. He did not hear my mother's cries. He sank down, fell almost, onto the couch. I forced myself to go all through the house. I was as frightened as any old maid, but I forced myself to open doors, peer into closets, look under beds. Gradually my heart quieted. I went back to the living room and found my mother fearfully peering in through the front door. My father was asleep.

"There's no one here, Mother," I told her. "Not a sign of anyone. You must have left the door open when we left."

She denied it, but eventually I was able to distract her, to calm her down with warm milk and mild talk.

I tried to describe this incident to Martha. Sitting with her in that dirty Third Avenue bar, I tried to re-create for her the horror of that moment: "You can't imagine," I said, "how ghastly it was standing there while Daddy rushed toward the house, toward that open door, and Mother stood there hysterical, absolutely hysterical with fright."

"Mmmm," Martha said vaguely. "Oh, I meant to ask you, could you and David come to dinner some night before you move?"

She thought *I* was hysterical. She was trying to distract

me, to calm me. I used hot milk with mother; she was using a dinner invitation with me. But I was not hysterical.
My mother is her mother, too. I wanted her to know
what was happening to our mother. I did not know how
much longer she could sustain that degree of tension.
Why didn't Martha want to listen to me? Because hys-
teria is not a polite subject. One does not discuss it. One
does not get angry at waiters or talk about hysterical
women or nervous breakdowns. Again, I could hear her
discussing me with her husband: "She went on and on,
with some wild story about burglars and Mother screaming on the street. Who knows what really happened? I
changed the subject as soon as I could."

We paid our checks. We each kissed the air, our
cheeks for a moment touching. We agreed it had been
lovely having lunch together.

That night, David said, "How was your lunch with
Martha?"

"Oh, fine," I said.

"Good," he said. "I'm glad you're getting out some.
It's good for you."

Victoria, usually so reticent, came home from the
park the next day with an anecdote: "We saw Mrs. Less-
ing and Dee-Dee in the playground. They were way over
on the other side when we came in, and Larry shouted,
'Dee-Dee!' and Dee-Dee said, 'Larry!' and they ran toward each other, and then when they met, they just stood

there. Just stood there and looked at each other without a word. Kids are so funny."

But don't we all do that? Run wildly toward a friend with outstretched arms, only to let them fall limply to our sides just before the point of contact? Wasn't my meeting with my sister Martha as noncommunicative as Larry's and Dee-Dee's? And why have I no recollections of seeing my older sister Sara during that month and a half before we moved? It seems unlikely that she would have failed to come to see me, to check on my progress, since she lives only an hour from New York. I have asked David about this, but he cannot remember either. It was such a confusing time, he says.

Sara must have come. She takes her role of eldest daughter seriously. Why shouldn't she? For she was, from an early age, more than the eldest daughter. Deified in the worshiping eyes of Mother, she became our household god. Whatever Sara did seemed to Martha, Mother, and me glamorous, exciting, adventurous. We were the stay-at-homes. She sallied forth on her adventures (dances at officers' clubs, dinners in elegant restaurants, weekends at country houses) and returned to hold us spellbound with her tales. Oh, Mother yelled at her, of course, for staying out too late, for spending too much money on clothes, for sleeping all morning, for not cleaning up her room, but all her admonishments failed to cover her admiration. Land's sake, the things that girl won't do! Wearing slacks to school! And purple lipstick! She'll be the death of me yet!

But she was not. Sara was the life of Mother. Mother lived vicariously through Sara's adventures and yawned over the dull procession of good report cards Martha and I brought home. She had two daughters who were stick-in-the-muds, but one at least had *get-up-and-go!*

And get up and go was precisely what Sara did. To Mother's chagrin, Sara went off to New York and never returned home to live. She married, conventionally enough, a scientist, and lives, conventionally enough, in a university town near New York. And to make matters worse, Sara even managed to prod Martha and me away from home. Martha went to New York after college, to work, and I to go to school. Like Sara, we never returned home.

I am grateful to Sara for her influence. Without her, I might have remained, suffocating, in the South. While I was going to school in New York and later while I was working there, I spent many of my weekends and holidays with Sara and her family. It was good to have a home to go to for Christmas, Thanksgiving, Easter, being, as I was, so far from home. But it was not good that Sara became a surrogate mother to me at an age when I should have no longer needed a mother. Sara always told me, for instance, exactly what she thought of any man I was seeing or clothes I had bought or hairstyles I had chosen to adapt. "That dress doesn't do a thing for you," she would announce, and I would find that despite the fact that I thought I disagreed with her, I would seldom wear the dress after that. It bothered me that I cared so much what she thought. After I started seeing Dr. Stern, I deliberately set out to free myself, to establish myself as an equal. I have hurt her, I know, by the clumsiness of my attempts. People receiving psychotherapy often do this: slash out too vehemently or at an inappropriate moment. I'm sure she liked me better before I saw a psychiatrist.

If she came to see me during my convalescence, and I have forgotten the visit, it is perhaps because I was ashamed before her. Sara thinks the purpose of life is pleasure. She has always regarded Martha and me as hopelessly inept in the art of living. She laughs at us for reading Gesell and Spock, yawns when Martha mentions her Brownie Pack, grows distant when I talk of my writing or courses I am taking. Life is fun and games; I had broken the rules by breaking down. Sara probably came to see me but acted as though nothing at all unusual had happened. I wish I could talk to my sisters. I miss them.

I telephoned Joan, waiting until after twelve to call because she usually stays in bed all morning. Because I felt as though I had been away at least six months rather than one, I found that I wanted to see all of my old friends, to renew my intimacy with them, before I moved to the country.

Joan sounded pleased to hear from me. But when I asked if I might come over, she hesitated.

"Oh, if you're busy, we'll make it another time," I said quickly. "Are you working on your book now?"

"It's not that. I'm not doing anything. The book's done—now I just have to sell it."

"Wonderful! Good luck! But you have plans, then, for this afternoon?"

"No—it's, well, it's that my brother's here. You remember Billy. His wife has left him. He's terribly depressed and—well, he doesn't want to see you. We were going to call you the other night, but Billy said he'd rather not be around you now."

Joan has always been frank. I thought this was rather overdoing it. "Oh, well," I said lightly, "it doesn't matter. I'm sorry about Billy. You call us when you have a chance—we certainly want to see you before we leave."

After I had said good-bye to Joan, I sat at my desk for a while feeling depressed myself. I decided to go out and buy myself some ice cream, pistachio, if I could find it, by way of compensation. If I could not have the adult pleasure of alcohol because of the medicine I took, it seemed necessary to regress to cake and candy and ice cream.

With Victoria taking care of the children all day, there was really very little for me to do except pack, and there were so many things that I could not pack until the last day or so because we would still be needing them. David thought I should be getting on faster with the job. But I felt in such a state of inner upheaval that I did not like to be reminded that in a few weeks all externals would change also. So one day, instead of packing, I called Alice and wangled an invitation to lunch. I wanted to see her before we left—and I felt a desire to be in a clean and orderly atmosphere. I could always count on Alice for that.

Alice is a Golden Delicious apple of a woman, with thick blond wavy hair, big soft brown eyes, a round welcoming figure, and a mind that is logical and quick: what is generally known as a masculine mind. When she opened the door, she was smoking a cigarette through a tortoiseshell holder; her shift dress, of gold silk knit, followed the lines of her body. While kissing her on the cheek, I noticed how much weight she had lost since she and Stan split up: she looked svelte rather than ample.

"Just a sec . . . I'll turn the set down," she said. I followed her into the apartment: a typical two-and-a-half-room East Side luxury apartment, but with the help of Sloane's and Altman's she had made it inviting, individual. Cool jazz, moiré music, the room shimmered with it, seductive sound, like ice clinking in a drink, piercing as the prick of an icicle. Cool jazz? Usually she played Vivaldi or Purcell or Handel.

But Alice had changed; she, too, was beginning a new life; hers, a sexy, jazzy, single life. She had divorced her husband of ten years; she had quit her job in advertising. She had had her hair, which formerly she wore in a matronly bun, cut so that it swung on both sides of her face into what hairdressers call a "flip." She had even changed her style of dress.

In winter she used to wear mostly woolen dresses knit by her mother, dresses that somehow made you think of Care packages and Bundles for Britain and refugee camps, even though her mother's craft was crafty enough. In summer she had favored cotton shirtwaist dresses. Once she showed up at our Fire Island beach house wearing a blue and white checked gingham one. Maureen, campy in white chinos and a sweat shirt from an Army-Navy store, kept grabbing me and saying, "But she's wearing a *house dress!* On Fire Island! A *house* dress!" Now Alice bought slacks from Jax and little fringed frocks from faggy East Side shops, and mid-calf suede boots for shopping and gallery hopping. She saw her psychiatrist three times a week, and the rest of the time she devoted to the pursuit of pleasure—intellectual, creative, or otherwise. Watching her as she moved across the room, I suddenly wondered what it would feel like to have an affair. I have been married forever.

"Would you mind turning it off?" I said.

"Of course not. Don't you like cool jazz?"

"At times. I'm not in the mood for it now."

She curled up in her favorite chair—it's just like our orange one, except that hers is covered in a greenish-gold fabric. She always sits there when I visit her, and I always sit on the couch, which is slipcovered in silk: white silk with thin stripes of gold, green, and orange.

She always curls up like a sleepy cat, and I always sit quite properly on the sofa and wonder how it stays so clean. Of course she has no children to jump up and down on the pillows or grind cookie crumbs into the cloth. An ample lap, full breasts, but no children.

"You're looking very well," she said. "I love your blouse!"

"This? Oh, thank you. But *you*, you really look sensational."

She picked up some needlework from the table beside her. "Let me show you what I'm making."

She is always making something: a sweater, or an eyeglass case, or booties for a friend's baby. This time it was a footstool cover in petit point: a traditional floral pattern worked in "contemporary" colors: orange, gold, tobacco brown, chartreuse. "Isn't it beautiful?" she said.

It would have been more agreeable of me merely to have said yes. Something prompted me to say instead, "Well, yes, you've done it very well—but I don't like petit point."

She was a little put out. "Why not?"

"Oh, I guess it reminds me too much of home. I mean, *everybody* had petit point all over the place."

She shrugged. "Well, I didn't grow up with it—I guess that's why I like it."

She is from a poor family in Brooklyn, but now she lived on the East Side of Manhattan and had a silk cover on her couch and a thick carpet on the floor and hundreds and hundreds of books in the bookcase that cov-

ered the wall behind her huge handsome desk and a
gold silk shower curtain in her bathroom and transpar-
ent Pears soap in the soap dish and her combs and hair-
pins were tortoiseshell and the bathmat was thick and
fluffy and golden and in her tiny, efficient kitchen the
pots were made of heavy copper, without a dent or
scorchmark.

She put down the needlework and almost reluctantly
turned her attention to me. "Speaking of home—how
are you? I haven't seen you since that one time right
after you got back—now, you *seem* fine . . ."

"I saw you after I got back?"

"Yes. Don't you remember? I came over—you talked
for hours about your trip—you were wild—I mean,
you were really turned on! Like Stan used to get sometimes, only more so—"

"I don't remember that at all." I wanted to ask her:
Did you know I was having a breakdown? But I didn't,
because she is a trifle smug about her knowledge of psychiatry, and it is easy enough to say yes after the fact.

"Really? Nothing at all?" She regarded me with that
fascinated stare most people gave me when they realized the extent of my memory loss.

"No. Nothing. What did I talk about?"

"Oh, God! Everything! One thing I remember is, the
husband of one of your friends had called you and offered
to be a pallbearer when your father died. You said,
'That's what friends are like at home. Nobody in New
York would think of such a thing.'"

"That's true, isn't it?"

"I suppose, yes." She smoothed back her hair in a gesture that is peculiarly hers: using the heel of her hand rather than her fingertips. "But people can be good friends here too. They do things for each other."

The subject of friendship didn't really interest me. I was trying to think who the prospective pallbearer might have been. Patricia's husband? That seemed likely.

She bent down and picked up a piece of knitting from a wicker workbasket that sat on the floor near her chair. "I'm making a sweater for my cousin's baby." She paused, then went on somewhat warily, as though addressing someone who knew only a little English. "Do you—do you remember when I tried to teach you how to knit?"

I had tried to learn how to knit? I hunched forward, frowned, with enormous effort produced the appropriate memory, then relaxed back against the soft cushions of the couch as the episode unrolled in my mind.

I was pregnant and had got it into my head that it would be a good thing for David, in the evenings, to look up from his reading and see his round-bellied wife placidly purling away at some sort of knitted garment for his unborn child. Alice came over several times and gave me lessons. She cast on, then I knit a few inches with a ball of used wool. I have long, slender fingers that look as though they should be dextrous. Eventually, Alice said, "Well, look, if you're not enjoying it, there's no reason why you should go on with it. Not everybody likes knitting. Maybe it's just not for you."

"I think you're right," I said, happy to have my doubts confirmed by her.

Her needles clicked, a steady sound, comforting as the tick-tock of a clock. Whatever she was making, it would turn out well. Her marriage had failed, her womb was empty, but her apartment was clean and fragrant and unflawed. I felt drowsy, from the Elavil, probably. I wished I could go lie down on her bed and take a nap.

I yawned. "Yes, I do remember. But it seems like ages and ages ago."

After lunch (sardines on stale bagels: she exudes *gemütlichkeit,* but keeps her cupboards bare as Mother Hubbard's), we had a cup of tea, followed by sherry and more chitchat. I thanked her and left, promising to call her before we moved. Later, at home preparing dinner it pleased me to see how well stocked my own kitchen cabinets were.

"What are you thinking about?"

I was sitting in a comfortable armchair strategically placed a few feet from Dr. Stern's chair and close enough to the low bookcase so that the patient could easily reach out for a tissue from the box that was always on the top shelf of the bookcase. I, however, had no need for a tissue: I felt brittle and bored rather than weepy.

I sighed. Was it worth explaining? I remembered the woman in Penelope Mortimer's book *The Pumpkin*

Eater who, when asked the same question by her psychiatrist, replied succinctly, "Dust." How could any man understand how much of a woman's life is spent thinking about dust? But if I told him I was thinking about another woman in a book who thought about dust, we would get distracted into a discussion of that book. What I wanted to talk about was not the book but the dust itself—or, in my case, grease.

"Well?" he demanded.

I studied the fingernails of my right hand. They needed cutting. "I am thinking about grease."

"Grease?" He lifted his eyebrows. We had been talking about what had happened since he had last seen me: how I was proceeding with plans for moving, how my husband's business was going, the people I had seen, until I lapsed into the long silence that he finally broke with the psychiatrist's classic question.

"Yes, grease. You see, there are grease spots all over the wall behind my stove. I can't get them off. I know it shouldn't bother me, because we're moving very soon, but it does. First I scrubbed the wall with a detergent. When the wall was still wet, I thought, aha, I've got rid of them all, but when it dried, there they were again, every single one of them. Then I tried Mr. Clean, full strength, like it says on the bottle, but the spots are still there. It's always the same: wherever I live there are grease spots all over the kitchen wall."

"Why do you think that is?"

"I don't know. There's something wrong with me.

Other women know what to do about grease, but I don't. David says, 'Maybe other people don't serve fried food,' but I know they do—they have me over for dinner and we have things like fried chicken and fried potatoes, but no one else has grease on their kitchen walls."

"How do you know? Maybe you just don't notice it. You know you're bound to notice flaws in your own housekeeping before you see them in other people's."

"Well, lately, whenever I go to someone else's apartment, I make sure I get into the kitchen so I can look for grease. I ask if I can help or if I can get a drink of water, and when I get to the kitchen, I look for grease spots, but there never are any—well, never any to speak of. Not like in my kitchen. Alice's kitchen, for instance, is immaculate. I was there the other day, and I mean it was *pristine*."

"Why are you so hard on yourself?"

I sighed again. I looked away from him, not wanting to meet his gaze. Sometimes I wished I were lying on the couch instead of sitting in a chair, so that I would not have to meet his eyes. Yet I was the one who had chosen the chair. "I don't know," I said irritably. What help was it to raise that question again? I would gladly pay twenty dollars to find out how to get rid of the grease spots, but he did not know the answer to that problem, any more than he knew why I was so hard on myself. He did not need to know about grease spots. He was a man, a psychiatrist. All that he had to do was sit in his chair and listen and now and then interject a question: Why are you so hard on yourself? Why indeed?

"In a sense, you are right when you claim that your treatment has been a failure. You still have so much self-hatred. I don't know why we haven't been able to do more about that."

I was listening but thinking my own thoughts at the same time. I was remembering the last time I had gone to a museum with David. We had gone to a retrospective show of the work of Jasper Johns, at the Jewish Museum.

We stood before a large canvas depicting a target. Across the top of the canvas, set in a narrow box, were six sculpted heads. I stared at the painting. David, having looked long enough to satisfy his interest, moved toward the next painting. Not noticing that he had left me, I remained before the target.

"Do you like that one? What are you thinking so hard about?" David said, returning to my side.

"Nothing," I said, moving on to the next painting. How could I tell him that my thoughts did not concern the painting at all? Jasper Johns had bought a canvas and squeezed oil paints out of tubes and applied it to brushes and brushed the paint onto the canvas and washed out his brushes with turpentine and put them away and mixed water with plaster of paris and sculpted the head of a man, six times, the same head, and then he had made a long narrow box to hold the heads and fastened the box to the canvas: all of this because he had something to say. What he had to say was ironic and humorous and perhaps even profound, and I, an upper-middle-class, college-educated wife, stood before his work transfixed and thought: I have lamb chops. If we get home in time to defrost them. Salad . . . I have enough. Home-fried potatoes or a frozen vegetable? He'd like home-fries better—we'll have to stop for milk.

Grease. More grease. My life: no oil paintings, no plaster of paris heads, no sculpted monuments to mankind. I had not done any writing in months. Dust. Grease. Empty milk bottles. More grease. Finally, ashes.

"It's time to stop, now," Dr. Stern said. "I'll see you Thursday."

Why? I thought. Why bother to come back? On the other hand, why not? "All right," I said.

On the way home I thought: How strange. I didn't even mention my breakdown today. Perhaps the period of mourning is over. I can get back to my normal, lifelong problem: how to be a woman without hating yourself for being only a woman.

Eventually I began to realize that in many ways my breakdown must have been harder on David than on me. During the month that I was in the hospital, I was oblivious to the reality of the situation. He was the one who had to worry about the mounting hospital and doctor bills, while I sat around saying, "I want a private room! I want to go home!"

He must have wondered if I would actually recover in a month as the doctors predicted. Knowing that psychiatry is an inexact science, he must sometimes have had to deal with the frightening possibility that my illness might last for months, even years. He told me that one day he was so anxious that he called both Dr. Rosen and Dr. Stern and asked them if he shouldn't just forfeit his deposit on the house. "I said, 'Surely she won't be in any shape to move by then.' They both said absolutely not to worry and not to consider giving up the house."

In talking about that month, he tries to minimize his difficulties; he doesn't want me to become depressed or overladen with guilt. But I do not have to be told to know what an ordeal it was. He loves to sleep late, but while I was away, he had to get up at seven thirty or so to change and feed the children. Then he had to work all day, taking off only enough time to visit me, and after work come home to the clamorous demands of two babies who had to be played with, then changed again and put to bed. Then a lonely dinner and a few hours' vigil before the TV set (he said he was too upset to concentrate on serious reading) before he could go to bed, to a bourbon-induced sleep.

Of course, our friends helped. Elaine Green came over one night and stayed with the children while David had dinner at her place with Jim. An old friend of David's came over several times for chess and darts. Quite a number of people called to offer to help in any way they could. Even the neighbor who professed to be terrified of children came up one evening to sit with the children so that David could visit me because he had been too busy to go in the afternoon. And one of our dearest friends called one day and said, "I know this kind of thing costs a lot. I can help you out if you need money. I can let you have, say, up to a thousand." It was a generous offer. He isn't a rich man and he has his own family to look after.

Weekends were the worst. Victoria was off then. David had the children all to himself, except for the times when his mother came to help. "Believe me," he said, "I was better off taking care of them alone. All she did was follow them around with a spoon trying to make them eat!" Despite such remarks, David is very fond of his mother, and more like her than he realizes. I wondered what my children would say about me when they were grown.

My friend Charlotte collects boxes. Small, decorative boxes of silver and china and various woods. She doesn't keep anything in them: she just lines them up on the living room mantelpiece. Once a week she dusts them. The maid is not allowed to handle them.

During my convalescence I collected famous people who have been touched by madness. Virginia Woolf (try not to remember that she committed suicide). Emily Dickinson. Van Wyck Brooks. Tolstoi. I was surprised to learn one day that I could add Robert Lowell to the list. Reading a review of a recent book of his, I had been thinking that he was a man who has had a good life. He started out with the advantage of a distinguished background and he profited from it. How jarring it was to learn then that he has been in mental hospitals several times.

Dr. Stern said, mocking my shame, "Why, it's almost a sign of genius to have a breakdown."

But I had the sign without the genius. It was quite foolish of me to derive reassurance from my collection. Yet it's a hobby no worse than collecting empty boxes.

One afternoon Martha telephoned to see how I was, but I barely managed to say "fine" before she began talking about her son's current problem in school. He was afraid of failure so he didn't try very hard. She was pleased that the teacher had called her. "She's really a good teacher. She's so aware of what's going on in the class."

She went on then to talk about the importance of good schools for your children from the very first grade. She'd heard the schools in our area are not very good. She thought I should seriously consider private school for the children. I was only half listening; my children were such babies. For them, school seemed centuries away.

"You'll find out," she warned. "If you don't get them off to a good start, you'll be in trouble later on. My friend Sheila Ward found that out with her little girl. Jenny had a teacher who'd had a nervous breakdown

when she was in third grade, and when they moved to
Greenwich the next year, Jenny couldn't keep up. She
had a terrible time." Her voice was surprisingly indig-
nant as she pronounced the words "nervous breakdown."
In the brief moment before she continued I thought:
Now she'll realize what she said and get all embarrassed
and try to make amends with some comforting phrase
like, "Of course, I mean a *serious* one, not like yours."

To my astonishment, when she continued, she repeated her remarks, as though she really wanted to rub
it in: "This teacher had a *nervous breakdown,* and of
course the schools in Greenwich are so good that Jenny
really had a difficult time."

She went on talking, but I stopped listening. I was
trying to puzzle out why she should have said such a
thing to me, not once, but twice. Had she so insulated
herself from my illness and its possible threat to her (is
there a weakness perhaps in the family strain?) that she
actually did not remember as she spoke that I too have
had a breakdown and could not therefore enjoy her remarks, which seemed to imply that one could not recover
from a breakdown and return to a normal, useful life?
Or was it an expression of unconscious hostility, a subtle
way of telling me she thought me irreparably damaged?

Gradually I became aware of my improvement. The
air was clearing after the storm. Someone—I don't remember who it was—said to me shortly after I left the
hospital: "You have a rosy future." I thought then: You

don't know. You don't understand that I am enveloped by a thick gray fog. Now that the fog was vanishing, I could agree with that unknown person. We were going to live in the country with our children. We'd raise apples and pears and plums; corn, squash, tomatoes, peppers; sturdy farmyard flowers: zinnias, marigolds, sunflowers, hollyhocks. We'd watch the slow change of seasons, the fire of the setting sun on snow, the silver of the rising moon on fields of hay.

Nothing had changed since the previous week, or the week before that, yet everything had. Until the fog lifted, I could not see the view. Suddenly, its beauty astonished me.

It sometimes troubled me that perhaps I owed my contentment to the pill I took each morning. Parnate, it was called. (The Elavil made me too drowsy.) It was tiny, red, round as the sun. I swallowed it: my interior landscape grew radiant.

I did not know how much longer I would be permitted to take these pills. Dr. Stern talked of possible side effects. At times my new confidence wavered. If the pills were withdrawn, would the fog roll in again? At other times, I thought not. The metaphor of the storm was apt. I had survived an electrical storm.

My mother was afraid of lightning and thunder. When a storm broke, she showered us with warnings: Don't sit by an open window or a fireplace. Don't take a bath. Don't use needles or scissors or knives. If you do, you'll be struck by lightning!

She was right.

She prophesied my future.

Her warnings are woven into the tissue of my brain; they circulate through the blood of my body.

I disobeyed her: I used a knife during a storm. I stretched out on a table and parted my legs and said to the doctor, "Cut!"

He cut, and two minutes or two months later—what does it matter?—lightning struck.

Another man fastened electrodes to my forehead: cold metal plates. Lightning struck: my body twitched with convulsions.

All right, Mother, you told me so. (I had suffered. I had atoned.) The storm was over. The sun was shining again. I was ready to go out to play—with or without her permission.

I saw Dr. Stern again. I told him some of the thoughts I had been having concerning my breakdown, and almost timidly expressed my belief that I was perhaps now "weller than well." He smiled and said, "You seem almost afraid to tell me that," but did not comment further or evaluate my belief. I went on to describe my sense of loss at being deprived of any memory of the manic episode and almost all memory of the hospitalization. "I feel now that I might be able to learn something from the experience, if only I could remember it." I told him that in this respect, I didn't think shock treatment was a very satisfactory treatment. He agreed, and then after we

had talked some more about shock treatment and why I
had needed it, he made an astonishing suggestion: "Why
don't you go back and visit the hospital?"

I was so startled that for a few moments I merely stared
at him. My nonthinking response was: "Oh, I couldn't."

"Why not?" he asked.

"I'd be frightened."

"But why?"

My unsatisfactory answer: "I don't know." The
thought was so alarming that I preferred not to think
about it, not to try to analyze why it was frightening.

"As an author, you would probably be allowed to
visit," he said.

As an author! I was delighted to be called an author
by him. I had been reasonably successful as a copywriter,
but for my other writing I had only rejection slips.

After I left Dr. Stern's office, I went to Bloomingdale's
to buy undershirts and pajamas for the children, and
while I was doing this, I found myself thinking: Why
not go back to the hospital? Perhaps all those days will
come rushing back.

But did I really want them to? Or was I afraid to face
them?

Another possibility was that I might go back and remember nothing more than I already did. If I go, I
thought, and merely look around and think, oh, so that
is what the building looks like, I see. I walked in through
that door and here is the lobby and over there is the admitting room and I sat down in that chair and talked to

that woman, if all I see are furniture and people and walls and files and doors, what good will it do? It will contribute nothing at all to my understanding of the experience for me to add all those details to my memory.

Anyway, I decided, I'm too busy to go. There isn't time before we move. Yet I think that Dr. Stern's suggestion may have had something to do with my eventual decision to write this book.

My resentment at having received shock treatment was increasing. My conscience had always been too powerful. During the manic state, I stifled part of it. But why wasn't I allowed to be free a little longer? I began to wonder. Even a common laborer gets a two-week vacation. I was manic for four days and then was locked up in a hospital. I have the stigma now: I've been hospitalized. But I never got to kick, scream, curse, or flaunt authority. They quieted me, shocked me, so that I returned immediately to my usual docile state.

I did not feel proud that I had been a "good" patient. They said now we will play bingo so I played bingo and won a chocolate bar. Why didn't I say to hell with your childish games? I thought that I was participating in the activities because boredom drove me to it. Not true. I did it because I was expected to. My breakdown might have been more therapeutic if it had not been controlled so rigidly and so rapidly.

My treatment with Dr. Stern had in some respects been a failure also. I didn't remember seeing him in the hospital, but judging from what he told me, I had as usual been a little girl, eager to please. During my visits to him after my hospitalization, I sometimes experienced a sense of depression because at heart I was the same good girl I had always been.

I was always on time or early for my appointments. When he opened the door, I smiled at him, no matter how I was feeling. I commented on his new suit or his new tie or the new painting in his office. All very proper, very "social."

One day he made coffee for us, and after I took the first sip, he said, somewhat anxiously, "Is it all right?"

"Delicious!" I said. It wasn't. The only thing delicious about it was that he had made it and handed it to me and wanted me to enjoy it. Actually it was lukewarm, and I like my coffee hot. Really hot. I wanted my hours with him to be hot also. Passionate. I wanted to be able to rage at him. I was able to be sarcastic. I could argue with him, using logic, but those techniques were too sophisticated. There was in me a more primitive urge that longed for expression.

It was too late for that. We were friends. I couldn't rage irrationally at a friend. I might have been able to strike out more vigorously years ago when I first began seeing him, but I hadn't. Both of us were too careful. Perhaps it doesn't matter. Probably all civilized people have such urges at times. But since I was more timid than most people, the urges were perhaps stronger.

Even my breakdown was a timid one, a "nice" one. I

didn't run through the streets naked or attack my husband or do anything hostile or violent. The three delusions I had all sought to strengthen my links with others, not sever them. Dr. Stern was not only my doctor, he was also in love with me. Miss Harding was not only my past employer, but also my cousin. Joan was not only my friend, but also my cousin.

How social I was! I saw two divergent ways of looking at this matter. One: I was so tightly corseted by my conscience that I couldn't break free even when I had a breakdown. Two: I was not as sick as those who express themselves more violently. My personality was mature enough so that I did not need to descend to such infantile levels. Of course, I preferred the latter interpretation. But if it was correct, why did I feel almost a sense of envy for those more violent, even though I knew that they suffered more than I did?

A bad evening. Helen came by for a few minutes. While she was with us, she mentioned a recent book that deals with abortion. David said that he had tried to read the book while I was in the hospital, but that he just couldn't get interested in it. "I guess I just don't think abortion is an important enough subject to write about."

I was sitting next to him on the couch, close enough to touch him with an outstretched hand. I had been married to him for ten years. So many hours and hours, aeons it seems, of talk! So many nights in bed with him! Yet we remained eternally separated by biology.

Abortion, it seems, is a woman's subject. Inferior. Birth and death, although fundamental, are relegated to the bedroom, traditionally the woman's room, although the man shares it. It is the "living" room that is reserved for real life, that is to say, *talking*. Of politics and money and philosophy. Real things. Masculine things. Nothing messily maternal occurs in the "living" room. (The name must have been invented by a man.)

I said nothing to David's remark as we sat there with Helen.

Later, in the bedroom, perhaps feeling freer once I was in my own domain, I told him that his remark had offended me. "After all," I said, "I had a breakdown because of an abortion. Do you expect me to consider it an insignificant event?"

He was hanging up his trousers. He completed the job of sliding them neatly over the wooden hanger before turning to me. "So you're accepting Dr. Stern's theory. You believe everything he tells you. Why can't you learn to think for yourself? Why do you have to keep going to *him* to find out what you think?"

I must remember, I told myself, that he is not immune to guilt. I must not shout out my resentment: your fault, your sperm, you who said wait, wait, so that I was old to be a mother, tired out by two pregnancies in two years. He, too, has suffered. Evenly I said, "I have tried to think. But I agree with Dr. Stern."

"It didn't bother you at all at the time. You never shed a tear."

"So?"

"So I'm going to watch television." Slam of the bedroom door. He fled from the bloody boudoir to the living room, to watch black and white images shifting about on the screen.

I lay awake for a long time thinking about the long years when I had wanted children but he had not; and of how, when he finally agreed, I did not conceive, as month after month passed. I went for all kinds of expensive and unpleasant tests to find out if anything was wrong with me. He finally had to be prodded, coerced into seeing the doctor, and it was he who had problems, not I.

That we actually did have children was a miracle. I don't think I would have been careless enough to conceive a third child by accident if we had not regarded the first two as miraculous.

In any case, I was sure now that I should not have had the abortion. I wondered why it had not occurred to me that even though the child was not wanted, I could have loved it. I was not my mother. Perhaps my capacity to love was greater than hers. History does not necessarily repeat itself. I thought then that I was creating my own morality. It is less immoral to destroy a child you do not want than to have an unwanted child and be unable to love it, I declared. My error was in not realizing that we cannot create our morality. It is thrust upon us.

More than a month had passed since my return from the hospital. I began to feel that I would never remember most of my stay there or what happened during my manic episode. Dr. Stern said that it was of no importance: "But it is one of the disadvantages of shock treatment. People dislike having loss of memory."

On a rational level I could agree with him. I knew it did not matter that I did not remember telephoning Miss Harding at five o'clock in the morning. It had nothing to do with my state of mental health then, which was satisfactory. The shock treatments had not damaged my mind. I was able to think as well as I had ever been able to (that is to say, not very well). But my *feelings* told me that my loss of memory did matter. Why was this?

I had always had a memory that was poor in some respects. For instance, I sometimes bought a book, thinking that it looked interesting, and then discovered, when I began reading it, that I had already read it. But that is not the same as forgetting *experiences*. I think that I forget a book I've read, if in reading it I have not *felt* it, been moved by it; in other words, if I have not experienced it. I believe it was Flaubert who used the term *felt life* in writing of Balzac's work. But it was Flaubert himself who was a master at creating felt life. Emma Bovary's death is unforgettable; it is almost as real to me as events in my own life.

A manic episode, I thought, should be unforgettable.

It is one thing to forget the name of someone you met at a party or a book that did not move you, but it is quite another matter to forget a month of your life, an extraordinary month.

Still I had not got any closer to deciding *why* loss of memory was so disturbing.

I went to the encyclopedia for help and was reminded that the term "memory" actually included two abilities: the ability to *retain* a past experience and the ability to *recall* it. ". . . some memories which affect personality are rarely recalled except through hypnosis or psychoanalysis." Well, in these Freudian days, we all know that.

I wondered how shock treatment affected the memory. Were the images of my manic days *retained* in my brain, although not recalled by me, or had they been destroyed by the electric shocks?

Why did it matter?

Because those days were mine.

They were unique.

No one living or dead had ever experienced a day just exactly like any one of them.

I am unique, I thought.

To myself, I am supremely important.

I did not want to be robbed of even one day of my life.

Why? Why did it matter?

My egotism was exposed, but the answer was not.

Is it because we know that our days are limited that we guard them so jealously?

A giant hand reached down and capriciously tore a

handful of pages from the calendar of my life. Where are they? Scattered to the winds.

My little boy said to me one day, "I don't like poo-poo." (Poo-poo was his baby word for feces.)

"Why not?" I asked.

"Because I can't eat it."

His poo-poo is his. He doesn't want to give it up. He wants to eat it, thus turning his digestive process into a circular one. Eat, make poo-poo, then eat the poo-poo, thereby making more, etc. A more satisfactory arrangement. If all the life processes were circular in structure, one might be able to live forever, without depending on others for nourishment.

I wanted my days back so that I could devour them. I didn't want them scattered to the wind or flushed down the toilet. I wanted them right where they belonged: in the cupboards of my mind, so that whenever I wanted to, I could open the cupboards and taste them again. Thus, you see, I could go on living forever. My days could not be "spent," could they, if I had them right there in my cupboard?

During the last days before we moved, the apartment was chaotic. The front hallway was lined with book cartons, filled, taped closed, and labeled. The kitchen, crowded with cartons of cookbooks, serving dishes, pots and pans, was an obstacle course. In the living room, cardboard china barrels, still folded flat, leaned against the empty bookshelves. It was impossible to forget that

we were about to disrupt our lives. It seemed to me that
I had never found packing so difficult. I suppose it was
because I did not really want to go anywhere then. There
was nothing that I desired more than the absence of
change, despite my occasional euphoric feelings that our
life in the country would be idyllic.

In the afternoon, between two and five, I showed people through the apartment. The superintendent would
have shown it, had I chosen to be out then, but I found
that I did not like the idea of people snooping through
my apartment while I was away. So I usually remained
home in the afternoon, and while it was a little annoy-
ing to have to keep jumping up to answer the bell, I
found that I rather enjoyed showing the place.

What were my own thoughts about moving? If I had
not felt that I needed more time to allow my wounds
to heal, would I have wanted to leave? I don't know. That
summer, the city seemed all right to me. On weekends,
the playgrounds were almost deserted. The days were
unusually clear and sunny. I liked walking along Third
Avenue and window-shopping for antiques. I liked looking at the paintings in the galleries on Madison, and
dropping into the Metropolitan Museum for a few minutes now and then. I would have been quite content to
stay on in New York. Instead, I woke up every morning
with a sense of uneasiness: Something is wrong. But what
is it? In a few seconds my mind cleared and I remembered. Two things were wrong. I had had a nervous
breakdown. And I had to move. Soon. Too soon.

*   *   *

I don't know how my friend Grace felt about the "going away" party she had for me, but I considered it a failure. A sense of sadness permeated the atmosphere. I first noticed it as I stood for a moment by a window in her living room, about an hour after we had arrived.

Her apartment is a floor-through in a brownstone, a charming place with high ceilings, sloping floors, and handsome marble fireplaces. She has furnished it with odds and ends of Victoriana set against lavender walls with white woodwork and juxtaposed to contemporary decorative touches: immense pink and lavender tissue paper flowers in an alabaster vase on the marble-topped dining table; a bronze abstract sculpture on the mantelpiece; between the two long living room windows, a painting of ballet dancers, sweetly absorbed in their own sweaty, tutued bodies. Standing there next to the painting, as self-absorbed, but less graceful than the ballerinas, looking out through one of the long windows at a plane tree growing in a sooty little court, I remembered a cemetery I used to visit as a child.

It was only three blocks from my house. I passed it on the way home from school. I used to stop in often, never alone, never on gloomy days. It was not a well-kept cemetery. The rows of tombstones leaned and slanted like a procession of the lame, the infirm, and the blind. Weeds overran the aisles and hid the faces of the tombstones like the matted hair of the mad. We used to search the stones for the graves of children. Finding a new one (one we had not seen before) gave me the same kind of bitter-sweet sensation I got from a spanking: after the sobs, what thumb-sucking joy to imagine yourself dying of a broken heart, your family weeping, repentant, at your grave! We would stand awestruck before the grave and solemnly read out the inscription: INFANT LEBLANC. SHE WAS WITH US BUT TWO DAYS BUT REMAINS IN OUR HEARTS AND IN HEAVEN FOREVER. BORN, APRIL 26, 1910. DIED, APRIL 28, 1910. Then, all in a rush, we bumped into each other, stumbled over our own feet, in a wild dash out of the cemetery. Last one out had to close the gate, had to drag that heavy, wrought-iron gate until it clanged: a sound to chill the blood on even the hottest of days. I can never forget that sound, or the smell of the cemetery, always the same: the scent of flowers, cut flowers in vases and flowers growing out of graves, mingled with the cold wet smell of stone and the nose-wrinkling stink of decay.

But why think of cemeteries when I was standing in a charming living room, dressed in my new beige silk, gold earrings dangling from my earlobes, an icy martini in my hand? A perfect martini, made with imported gin, imported vermouth, served in a chilled glass. On the marble-topped coffee table, a pâté from France, by way of Bloomingdale's, pickled mushrooms, artichoke hearts, stuffed vine leaves. Clever, charming people all around: art directors, copywriters, illustrators, filmmakers, all of them up on op and pop and space and race. Why think of cemeteries? Was it the presence of so much marble that put me in that urn-burial mood? Or the slant of the floor that linked that living room to the leaning stones of the dead? Or was it the way that plane tree pushed itself up through cracked cement with the vigor of a weed in a cemetery?

I didn't know. It was certainly not the proper mood for me to have at a party. I was the guest of honor. I should have been gala. I wasn't. My hands trembled. Even when I put my glass down, they felt cold. I stumbled on my sentences, let them trail off into vague confusions: "Well, I mean, I don't know if I made myself clear, what I mean to say is, oh, well, forget it." Maybe more alcohol would have helped, but I was not supposed to have more than one drink, so dutifully I limited myself to two.

I did try. I pulled myself away from that window, exorcised that cemetery, turned my mind fully on the guests, slid in and out of groups with almost my usual dexterity until suddenly I was struck still again with this thought: These people are all single. Tania, florid from too much to drink, overdressed as usual in her own style, which is a blend of Lillian and Rosalind Russell, has a child, but her husband is dead. Grace, despite her lovely Florentine face, has never married. That mocha, hand-carved Indian over there may be a bachelor because he is still young—or is there a shade too much of the scent of sandalwood about him? Johnny, I knew for sure, would never marry. His manner was neutral, rather than effeminate, but he didn't quite "pass." And so it went with them all—they were divorced, widowed, homo-

sexual, unwed—unwanted? Was it loneliness rather
than death I smelled?

No, no, no! The odor was not in that warm, tobacco-
filled, chatter-filled air, but in the putrid atmosphere of
my mind. How long must I go on being a pallbearer?

I left early, pleading tiredness, dragging a reluctant
David with me: "*Marvelous* party! I do so hate to leave—
but you understand, we have *so* much to do!"

The movers were supposed to come at eight. Surpris-
ingly, they appeared at eight, punctual to the minute.
Four big, bluff men. Just another working day for them.
For us, a milestone.

I, of course, woke up much too early: at six o'clock.
For a few seconds I tried to forget that it was an extraordinary day: a trick to woo the return of sleep. My
trick failed. I wanted to get up for coffee, but I was afraid
of waking the children, so I lay there listening to my
stomach rumbles and waiting for the alarm to ring.

Somehow I had managed to get everything done: the
washing machine and air conditioner sold to friends (and
actually picked up on schedule). Newspaper, laundry,
and diaper service discontinued. Con Ed and the telephone company notified. Everything packed. Endless
junk thrown out. The superintendent, already overworked, carried it off without complaint, no doubt in
expectation of a large tip.

Victoria came in at eight thirty with her suitcase. She
had agreed to stay with us in the country for two weeks,
to help us get settled. She fed the children amid the con-

fusion, then took them off to the park, just as though it were an ordinary day.

I wondered what Larry would say when he came back from the park and found his room empty and saw the familiar objects of his world being carried away by strangers. I had wanted to get the children away before the moving began, but since the men insisted on coming so early, I couldn't manage it. So we were scheduled to leave on the eleven o'clock train, go to Jane's for lunch; then, hopefully, the children would nap and I would go buy groceries for my new house.

My house. Our house. It was difficult to realize that the children would not even remember the apartment. Nor my breakdown. At least not consciously. Their memories of that period would be buried, like my memories of the month in the hospital.

I went into Larry's room to be out of the way. Then I felt as though I were hiding. I didn't like the sound of those heavy footsteps clumping through the apartment.

The movers wrapped thick, quilted pads around any furniture that needed protecting. They transformed the service elevator into a padded cell. I kept thinking of the men who came to get Blanche in the last scene of *A Streetcar Named Desire*. Did she have just a "breakdown," I wondered, or were you meant to think that she had gone totally mad? That's the trouble with works of literature: they end and you never know what happened afterward.

I knew what had happened to me. I had recovered.

There was no reason for me to hide. No one was going to lock me up. If I wanted to, I could walk out of there and go to the park. Or take a last look at Madison Avenue. It was a lovely day for a walk, a lovely day for moving: sunny, but not humid. From where I sat, I could see the other wing of the building and the big luxury co-op next door. An alley between the two buildings provided me with a narrow view of the sidewalk and the street and the small private house on the other side of the street, and above it, a strip of blue sky.

I raised the venetian blind (which was shamefully sooty) to have a better view. I saw two moving men carrying Larry's crib. For some reason, they set it down on the sidewalk, instead of carrying it into the van.

Then I saw Mildred, with Dee-Dee by the hand. They stopped beside the crib. Dee-Dee must have realized it was Larry's. Who else had a crib with orange and gold bars? I was too far away to hear their conversation, but I stood there watching them until they walked off toward the park. The movers took the crib into the van.

The next day when Larry woke up in his orange and gold crib, he would see fields and a barn and a silo and sky instead of this slit of a view, as pinched as that from a prison cell. Soon, I thought, he will be too big for his crib. Soon he will be able to climb out, to escape those bars whenever he chooses. To run free in the fields.

I hoped to God it would be so.

My children's freedom must not be bounded as mine was by the bars of childhood.

Epilogue

Most of this book was written shortly after I moved from New York City to our house in the country. Writing it was a catharsis for me. Simply setting down what happened helped me sort out my feelings about the strange episode that had taken place. I accepted the reality, although I did not like it.

When I had finished the manuscript, I made a few halfhearted attempts to find a publisher, attempts that were desultory because I was not even sure that I did want to publish it. At times I have felt it was far too personal a book for others to read. For a couple of years the manuscript lay in a drawer in my desk.

During these years, I had many other things on my mind. I was busy cooking, cleaning, entertaining friends and relatives, sewing name tags on sweaters and coats, teaching small fingers to tie shoelaces, wiping away tears, taking temperatures, explaining away bad dreams. I did not see my psychiatrist after the first few months in the country: his office was so far away and it began to seem that we had little of importance or fresh relevance to talk about. I stopped taking the medication I had been receiving. I did not very often think about that month in the hospital.

Yet it is always there in my past. As might a shadow on my lung or a murmur in my heart, it produces in me a fear not shared by everyone. To this day I do not completely understand why I had a breakdown. I can say yes, these were the causes, but still it seems to me extraordinary that I should have had this experience. My psychiatrist, too, was taken by surprise, though he could theorize after the fact. We have still so much to learn about how the mind works.

Eventually, I sent the manuscript out again, after adding to it some perspective gained during the past few years. Perspective. For me that may largely be the realization that I will never be the same person I was before my psychotic episode. Now I am consciously grateful for all that I previously took for granted. I remember, for instance, an incident which occurred two years before my breakdown, at a time when I had already had many years of psychotherapy, had written pamphlets on mental health, and had read a fair amount in the field of psychiatry.

My husband and I were staying that summer on Fire Island. Our neighbors had as a guest one weekend an attractive, vivacious girl who was an airline stewardess. Betty seemed a pleasant enough girl, if a bit on the superficial side. I remember watching her setting the

table and helping her hostess with the dinner and thinking then that she was a typical airline stewardess: always
smiling, always ready with a helpful hand. Betty must
have been about twenty-eight then. I wondered why
such a pretty girl was not already married.

A few weeks after we met Betty, our neighbors told us
that she was in Bellevue, that she had gone there herself
and asked to be committed, after doing some rather
strange things. Apparently a disastrous affair with a married man had precipitated her breakdown. I was surprised to hear this, but since I knew her so slightly, I
didn't think much about the matter.

One evening at the end of summer my neighbor said
to me, "Oh, I meant to tell you about Betty. She's all
right now. She's back at her job."

I said, "Really? You mean they took her back? Isn't
that a dangerous thing to do? What if she cracks up again?
And while she's working?"

"I know," my neighbor said. "I was surprised, too."
Our husbands joined us with drinks. We sipped them
and watched the sun submerge, smugly secure in our
sanity.

So this book is, to some extent, an apology to Betty.
I am sorry that my simplistic mind labeled her crazy
because she once spent three weeks in Bellevue. I am
ashamed of myself and astonished at my naïveté. I understand now that it is possible to recover from a psychotic
episode.

Unfortunately, not everyone has this knowledge. I

was reminded of this recently when someone asked me, "Do you consider yourself well now?" The question startled me. I had assumed that it was evident to all that I was in a satisfactory state of mental health. I thought for a few moments and then answered him as precisely as I could. "Well, obviously I'm not free of concern about the future. I'm sure if you've ever had cancer, you worry more about dying of cancer than a person who has never had it. Sometimes I wake up in the middle of the night and wonder if I'll ever be in a mental hospital again. But it gets better as time passes. Each year, when another June comes, I think, good, another year has passed. It's five years now since my month in the hospital. I feel less anxious than I did after one or two years. I'll feel even better when ten years have passed, still better after fifteen. I celebrate my wedding anniversary in May, another anniversary in June . . ."